D1415201

05/22/17

Excel. There is Room at
the top! Betterment
Pat Russell McHul Esq

My Journal:

Myself,
INSIDE OUT

CREATING THE PATH
PATRICIA RUSSELL-MCCLOUD, J.D.

Published by
LeTay Publishing
4153 Flat Shoals Parkway
Building C, Suite 332
Decatur, Georgia 30034
404-667-2810
booksales@letaypublishing.com
www.letaypublishing.com

My Journal: Myself, Inside Out

Copyright © 2013 by Patricia Russell-McCloud, J.D.
Layout and Design by ebentley Studio

The text for this book is Futura Light.
The cover art text is Viner Hand and Futura Bold.

PRINTED IN THE UNITED STATES

Library of Congress Cataloging-in-Publication Data
Russell-McCloud, J.D., Patricia
My Journal: Myself, Inside Out
Written by Patricia Russell-McCloud, J.D.

ISBN-13 978-0-9830731-2-3

1. Self-Help Techniques   2. Journal   3. Mind and Body
Ages 18 and up

$24.95

ANNOTATION

Knowing the real you takes courage and determination. Understanding who you are creates a doorway for you to construct ideas, build your plans and execute your dreams. A Best Selling Author and Acclaimed Orator for over 30 years, Pat Russell-McCloud, J.D. assists you in creating a path to your power and greatness with this journal. It features 365 days of inspirational and self-help techniques, as well as the space to explore your introspections.

DEDICATION

To all who need to celebrate themselves through enrichment,
empowerment and enlightenment. This is your day, week, month,
and year. Yes, this is your life.

PURPOSE

This Journal is to touch you at your point of need. It is to explore the sensitive life pieces on your journey, and to push you into being your best self-always. At once, this Journal will become your 'then and now;' the recordation of daily secrets, sacrifices and struggles, and the fact that you survived, even though, you thought that you would not. Tell your story, especially to yourself.

THIS JOURNAL IS TO TOUCH YOU AT YOUR POINT OF NEED.

Written by Patricia Russell-McCloud, J.D., President, Russell-McCloud & Associates, Atlanta, Georgia. Russell-McCloud is an international motivational speaker and author, "A is for Attitude: An Alphabet for Living" (HarperCollins), who celebrates 30 years as a master of her craft.

JANUARY

Attitude

"If you can't change your fate, change your attitude."
—Amy Tan

A WINNING ATTITUDE

SUNDAY:

Sunday: In life, you can strike out or you can hit a home run. For certain, you have to be in the game to play the game; and, once you learn to play the game, somebody will come along and move all of the bases. The question is how are you responding to the hand that life has dealt you? In other words, what is your attitude, good, bad or indifferent?

Reflection: Describe your attitude.

_____

_____

_____

_____

_____

_____

_____

_____

_____

_____

_____

_____

_____

_____

_____

_____

Believe in the impossible because no one else does, and that gives
me an excellent chance of achieving it.

A WINNING ATTITUDE

Attitude controls our lives. Be clear, that your attitude shapes your personality. Your personality sets the building block for the way you treat others, and how much you are able to accomplish. It ultimately depends upon what you believe.

Action Item: Whether, based upon your personality...you would like to meet yourself. If not, why?

_____

_____

_____

_____

_____

_____

_____

_____

_____

_____

_____

_____

Think about it...If you think that you are beaten—you are.

_____/_____/_____
Month   Day   Year

A WINNING ATTITUDE

TUESDAY:

Your attitude demonstrates how you will act towards those things you have to do. Are you a person who follows through or one who gives a commitment that is never fulfilled? Be responsible. Explanations are excuses. Practice making your word, your bond. Be certain to gain trust and respect from others as well as respect for yourself. Be dependable.

Action Item: Practice making your word your bond. Journal two instances when you kept your word and did what you said you would do. You may need to do less, and realize that you are one person, not several.

_____

_____

_____

_____

_____

_____

_____

_____

_____

_____

_____

_____

_____

The more you live, the less you die.

A WINNING ATTITUDE

Your attitude counts. If you have a plan, then stick to it, without insisting that your plans were derailed because of intervening causes. For example, an unexpected change in schedule, or other people saying that they would be involved and at the last minute they backed out. For all of these reasons and more, your good intentions did not complete the job. Don't find satisfaction in delaying to a tomorrow that is not promised.

Action Item: Complete two things that you were going to put off until tomorrow. How does it feel not to delay?

_____

_____

_____

_____

_____

_____

_____

_____

_____

_____

_____

_____

_____

Remember: Success actually embraces failure. It is that
recognition that makes you move forward to...the possible.

_____/_____/_____
Month   Day   Year

A WINNING ATTITUDE

THURSDAY:

Attitude is ever present within you. It is comparable to your daily personal signature. Your life will give you some joy, and some sorrows, some ups and downs, some rewards and frustrations, some victories and setbacks, but, through it all, you can win.

Action Item: What is your deepest disappointment? Identify your greatest victory.

_____

_____

_____

_____

_____

_____

_____

_____

_____

_____

_____

_____

It is true that leaders win hearts with love and compassion.

A WINNING ATTITUDE

Cancel the negative, which can range from being disappointed, disheartened, disenchanted, discouraged, or sometimes just dissed.

Action Item: Define your strategy for dealing with your emotional responses.

_____

_____

_____

_____

_____

_____

_____

_____

_____

_____

_____

_____

_____

Cancel the negative. Look for the win-win in positive situations.

_____/_____/_____
Month   Day   Year

A WINNING ATTITUDE

SATURDAY:

A good attitude is contagious. Share it. A negative attitude is also contagious. Be certain that you are not responsible for spreading its toxicity. Every exit is an entrance to some place else. Reject even the thought that you can't. Be determined that you can and you will. Be kind to others. Your quality of life will improve.

Reflection: Spread the positive. Cancel the negative.

_____

_____

_____

_____

_____

_____

_____

_____

_____

_____

_____

_____

_____

_____

Set the example with loyalty, integrity and follow through.

ATTITUDE ADJUSTMENT

An attitude adjustment will make the difference between failure and success, winning and losing, and whether you draw people to you or run them away. It is all in your attitude.

Action Item: On a scale of 1-5 (and 5 is outstanding!) how would you rate your attitude? List three reasons for your conclusion.

_____

_____

_____

_____

_____

_____

_____

_____

_____

_____

_____

_____

_____

_____

You can easily give up, and get weaker or guess what (!), you can forge ahead and excel.

9

ATTITUDE ADJUSTMENT

MONDAY:

How do you make an attitude adjustment? Your attitude is your thoughts and feelings about any situation. When you think and feel good about anything, you have a good attitude. When you think and feel bad, or hate doing something, your attitude will reflect that as well. To change your attitude you must change your thoughts, words, pictures and feelings.

Reflection: Identify a time or circumstance when you consciously adjusted your attitude.

_____

_____

_____

_____

_____

_____

_____

_____

_____

_____

_____

_____

While others get frustrated, you make a decision to get busy.

ATTITUDE ADJUSTMENT

Whether you react or respond to what happens is largely due to your attitude about that situation. Things happen. You cannot determine what will happen in your life and when or even how. Create the habit of making a positive attitude adjustment and watch changes that happen in your life.

Action Item: List three ways in which you can change your attitude.

_____

_____

_____

_____

_____

_____

_____

_____

_____

_____

_____

_____

_____

*Think about it...if you want to build,
work on your own foundation.*

_____/_____/_____
Month   Day   Year

ATTITUDE ADJUSTMENT

Wednesday:

WEDNESDAY:

Be certain that whatever tasks that you have, you perform them in an excellent manner. Make your presentations clear, concise and always follow up. Identify your priorities.

Reflection: Are you working to be your best self notwithstanding the fact that you know the material and your audience?

_____

_____

_____

_____

_____

_____

_____

_____

_____

_____

_____

_____

Refuse to send out 'holier than thou' attitudes.
Even eagles land sometime.

_____/_____/_____
Month   Day   Year

12

ATTITUDE ADJUSTMENT

Thursday:

Refuse to blame others or engage in activities that somebody else could have or should have done. Get your job done, without debate or delay.

Reflection: Identify whether and when you failed to take responsibility for a task that was actually yours.

_____

_____

_____

_____

_____

_____

_____

_____

_____

_____

_____

Attitudes are contagious.
Ask yourself whether yours is worth catching?

_____/_____/_____
Month   Day   Year

ATTITUDE ADJUSTMENT

FRIDAY:

Having a good attitude involves emotional hygiene. Be certain that you have the mind-set, mood, and behaviors that make you a desirable human being to be around. Stay in balance whenever there are situations, relationships or circumstances that are annoying, upsetting or get on your last nerve.

Action Item: How do you handle stress? List three strategies that keep you upbeat, encouraged and able to brush off that which would otherwise be upsetting.

_____

_____

_____

_____

_____

_____

_____

_____

_____

_____

_____

_____

You are not typecast in a specific role. Be you.

ATTITUDE ADJUSTMENT

Consider meeting another person halfway, you may need the exercise. Life doesn't last. Decide what is really important. Don't trade in your own happiness for being constantly angry. Take charge of the things that you can control. Learn from your stumbling blocks so that you are better prepared for any recurrence in the future. Life is hardball. Play ball.

Reflection: Think about the fact, that no one escapes life, alive.

Be determined...you can make a difference.
Remember at times you have to fake it until you make it.

15

_____/_____/_____
Month   Day   Year

GUILTY AS CHARGED

SUNDAY:

What do you stand for? What is your personal brand? Are you intellectual enough to answer a thought-provoking question? Do you also have the emotional intelligence to know when to stop fighting a battle going on in your life that it is not worth fighting, literally or figuratively?

Reflection: Who is it that you perceive yourself to be?

_____

_____

_____

_____

_____

_____

_____

_____

_____

_____

_____

Be clear on what you stand for.

GUILTY AS CHARGED

When someone takes you to the level of unbelievable disappointment, are you able to rise higher than their small and conniving ways, and be your better self? Take the high road.

Reflection: When did you demonstrate character and integrity when someone else sought to bring you down?

_____

_____

_____

_____

_____

_____

_____

_____

_____

_____

_____

_____

_____

Stand for something worthwhile.

_____/_____/_____
Month   Day   Year

GUILTY AS CHARGED

TUESDAY:

Be actively involved in leading a worthy cause. Demonstrate the acumen for strategic partnerships to show how important it is to work together and to set the example for the future, and for generations following. To do so, is an exercise in learning, commitment, productivity and not in finding and employing shortcuts. You may lose, win or draw, but at least you tried.

Action Item: List two projects when you have seen the benefit of working together to achieve the desired outcome.

_____

_____

_____

_____

_____

_____

_____

_____

_____

_____

_____

_____

_____

Life has choices. Based upon who you are,
what will you chose?

_____/_____/_____
Month   Day   Year

GUILTY AS CHARGED

Know where you are going, in fact. Don't pretend. You will encounter detours, and travel routes that will not get you where you intended to go.

Action Item: In mapping out your future, identify three critical destinations.

_____

_____

_____

_____

_____

_____

_____

_____

_____

_____

_____

_____

What does having courage really mean?

_____/_____/_____
Month   Day   Year

GUILTY AS CHARGED

THURSDAY:

You have the unmatched opportunity and mandate to participate in life. So, don't just think about it, or take notes on the events that are passing you by. Take a quantum leap forward and do your own thing. Always be your own priority and make a conscious decision to never be someone else's option.

Action Item: List two clear ways that you have made a decision to prioritize your personal goals and timetables.

_____

_____

_____

_____

_____

_____

_____

_____

_____

_____

_____

_____

Your beliefs and values will frame what you stand for.
It is an adventure worth your exploration.

GUILTY AS CHARGED

There is an urgency that requires us to do. Merely knowing is inadequate, we must do. One day at a time is enough. The past is gone. Do not worry about the future. Live in the present, everyday. Make it a treasured memory.

Reflection: Hold tight to the good days that come your way. If you placed that memory in a treasure box, what would it be?

_____

_____

_____

_____

_____

_____

_____

_____

_____

_____

Decide what this quote means:
"You can't understand another person until you walk a few
miles in their moccasins."
—Native American Proverb

_____/_____/_____
Month Day   Year

GUILTY AS CHARGED

SATURDAY:

Shutterfly asked this telltale question: "If death meant just leaving the stage long enough to change costumes and return as a new character...would you slow down or speed up?"

Action Item: Life has several stages. If you changed costumes, what would you be?

_____

_____

_____

_____

_____

_____

_____

_____

_____

_____

_____

_____

_____

Think about it...Is it important that you stand for more than honesty, integrity, empathy, tolerance, and dedication.

_____

HURT HURTS

Many tend to belabor their decisions, possible consequences, and scenarios until they resemble more of a mountain than a molehill. Once you are pushed into a corner, what happens to rational thought? Yes, it goes right out the window.

Action Item: Explain the value of thinking beyond emotional approaches and finding conclusions that address what is, rather than what you think it is.

_____

_____

_____

_____

_____

_____

_____

_____

_____

_____

_____

_____

Words, large or small, can hurt you or help you.
You decide.

23

HURT HURTS

MONDAY:

If it's not a fight-or-flight situation, stepping back and taking a deep breath can help you to get a more objective point of view. Become conscious of what you're feeling and what the other person could be reacting to at the moment.

Reflection: There is realism, optimism and the truth. Decide.

_____

_____

_____

_____

_____

_____

_____

_____

_____

_____

_____

_____

_____

Everyone has the power to hurt you.
It is their choice as to whether they decide to do it.

_____/_____/_____
Month Day Year

HURT HURTS

When you fall down, typically the first response is, 'Oh, I am fine. I am not hurt.' You do not want the attention or the embarrassment. You want to ache in private. Soon you will experience hurt, even more than the actual pain from the fall.

Reflection: In what situation did you 'act' fine, but you were actually devastated? How did you overcome?

_____

_____

_____

_____

_____

_____

_____

_____

_____

_____

Take a good long look at the people you are allowing to hurt you.
Ask yourself what you think of them.

_____/_____/_____
Month   Day   Year

25

HURT HURTS

WEDNESDAY:

There is no question that the existence of hurt, affects your being. Whether it is a grudge, an outright lie, or someone who brought joy to your life who now seems to be gone forever, you may seek a level of forgiveness that is long lasting and sincere.

Reflection: How did you feel when you let go of feelings of ill will and moved into the realm of mental, emotional and physical well-being?

_____

_____

_____

_____

_____

_____

_____

_____

_____

_____

Make it a habit to refuse to care about somebody else's private business. Handle your business and leave theirs alone.

HURT HURTS

When you talk about your hurt, you hurt less than if you decide to dwell in your own misery. Although some wounds may never heal, you must help yourself.

Reflection: Be cathartic. Let it go. Then take giant steps to reach your highest mark. Assume that you are moving from a season of discomfort to possibility.

_____

_____

_____

_____

_____

_____

_____

_____

_____

_____

_____

Accept it. Get over it. Everybody gets hurt.

_____/_____/_____
Month   Day   Year

HURT HURTS

Even after the pain of hurt, there is the relief of renewal. Maturity also comes with each encounter. Without seeking it or willingly making an acquaintance with hurt, life doesn't give you a pass. Instead, when you concentrate on yesterday, you will revisit the harsh words that were spoken, the acts of omission and/or commission; or your once thought to be best friend who crushed your very being. Move on.

Action Item: If others knew your then, they would keep you from your when. What strategies are you using to fly?

_____

_____

_____

_____

_____

_____

_____

_____

_____

_____

_____

_____

When a relationship doesn't work out the first time, so what?
You have choices. Decide.

HURT HURTS

It is possible and even true, that you can actually hurt the one you love. Furthermore, you can be hurt by the one who says that they love you. Love relationships present a slippery slope, so, your first step is to seek to determine what happened and why? That achievement is typically accomplished through listening. You don't have to forgive and forget, because it did occur. If you listen, you may learn how to avoid the repeated negative behavior of your significant other. Think the situation through, you don't ever need to be a victim. Being hurt, is neither your banner nor your burden.

Action Item: Make a list of the positive things about the person who hurt you. Now, what did that same person do to hurt you? Which list outweighs the other?

_____

_____

_____

_____

_____

_____

_____

_____

_____

_____

_____

_____

*"There is a thin line that separates laughter and pain,
comedy and tragedy, humor and hurt."*
–Erma Bombeck

29

Month   Day   Year

KEEP IT REAL

Let your lifetime achievements be those that show that you fought for what was right and fair, that you risked for that which mattered, and that you gave help to those who were in need. Make certain that you left the world a better place than you found it.

Reflection: Each week review your accomplishments. What grade would you give yourself?

_____

_____

_____

_____

_____

_____

_____

_____

_____

_____

_____

_____

_____

_____

Worry about your character and not your reputation.
Your character is who you are, and your reputation is only
what people think of you.

KEEP IT REAL

Temporary gains are not what you should seek in life, even though you will have more than a few opportunities to trade in your integrity for a quick fix on something fleeting.

Reflection: Set an example by being an example that is worthy of emulation.

_____

_____

_____

_____

_____

_____

_____

_____

_____

_____

_____

_____

_____

At times, you have to just be quiet, swallow your pride and consider another person's view. It is not called giving up. It is growing up.

_____/_____/_____
Month   Day   Year

31

KEEP IT REAL

TUESDAY:

Your word is your bond. Don't place yourself in a balancing act trying to please everybody by aimlessly making promises that you have no intention of keeping. Keep your commitments: whether it is serving on a committee or making the grade at school or at work or attending a work event. Your word is tied to your integrity. Gain the respect of others.

Action Item: List two times when you broke your promise and the resulting effect of your action.

_____

_____

_____

_____

_____

_____

_____

_____

_____

_____

_____

_____

_____

_____

Multi-tasking is the trend;
be certain to focus and accomplish one thing at a time.

KEEP IT REAL

Don't forget who you are, where you came from or where it is you plan to go. These lifelong components are connected, not mutually exclusive. Connect your past to your present and your future. It will make you a better person because you will find that you are not running from yourself.

Reflection: It is your life. Live it. Be a star in your own show and not an extra in somebody else's. Are you the main character?

_____

_____

_____

_____

_____

_____

_____

_____

_____

_____

_____

_____

_____

*If someone stands with you through the worst of times,
consider whether they also deserve to stand with you
during the best of times.*

_____/_____/_____
Month   Day   Year

KEEP IT REAL

THURSDAY:

Being pretentious is to make a poor choice. It does not take long for your friends, relatives or fans to recognize that you are phony, make believe and/ or that you avoid being truthful. Telling the truth is always the easiest path. Because once you tell the truth, you don't have to remember what you said.

Reflection: Quickly apologize for any hurtful actions.

_____

_____

_____

_____

_____

_____

_____

_____

_____

_____

_____

_____

_____

_____

_____

_____

*Set aside more of your time for your passions
and purposeful work.*

KEEP IT REAL

FRIDAY:

Bring closure to issues that may be pending between yourself and other people. Don't be confrontational. Be truthful, honest and comfortable in knowing that the person knows how you feel about a given situation.

Reflection: Live more in the moment.

_____

_____

_____

_____

_____

_____

_____

_____

_____

_____

_____

_____

Enjoy more of nature's company.

_____/_____/_____
Month   Day   Year

KEEP IT REAL

SATURDAY:

Volunteer your time and give service to others. Make certain that you engage in a simple pleasure every day.

Reflection: If you really want to make a difference in your life, make a difference in the lives of others.

_____

_____

_____

_____

_____

_____

_____

_____

_____

_____

_____

_____

_____

_____

_____

Be grateful for what you have, what you can do,
and for everything in your life.

FEBRUARY

Self-Awareness

"Breathe. Let go. And remind yourself that this very moment
is the only one you have for sure."
—Oprah Winfrey

YOUR BUCKET LIST:
CREATE A LIST OF THINGS TO DO BEFORE YOU DIE

SUNDAY:

Think about it. You are probably ready to begin creating your bucket list. That is, the things you want to do, places you want to see, people you want to meet, food you want to eat, and the list goes on, before you literally, kick the bucket.

Reflection: It is your list, so be adventuresome, without restrictions. You can break the paradigm, move past the status quo and step outside of your comfort zone. Enjoy.

_____

_____

_____

_____

_____

_____

_____

_____

_____

_____

_____

_____

_____

Always keep your goals.
If needed, make adjustments as to how you meet them.

YOUR BUCKET LIST:
CREATE A LIST OF THINGS TO DO BEFORE YOU DIE

MONDAY:

It is your special fortune that 'the world is your oyster.' You can do whatever you want to do. Stretch.

Reflection: Take your time. Think of the opportunities that can be yours if you are willing to take on the adventure.

_____

_____

_____

_____

_____

_____

_____

_____

_____

_____

_____

_____

_____

Think of the formula that gives you the great equalizer
—exposure.

_____/_____/_____
Month   Day   Year

YOUR BUCKET LIST:
CREATE A LIST OF THINGS TO DO BEFORE YOU DIE

TUESDAY:

Your Bucket List is your blueprint to be turned into your reality. To make your list happen will require your willingness to take ownership of the fact that it will require action, your participation and your anticipated long term good memories because you were bold and courageous enough to take the steps for your future.

Action Item: Ensure that there are at least five countries outside of the United States that you add to your Bucket List. List them.

_____

_____

_____

_____

_____

_____

_____

_____

_____

_____

_____

_____

Wherever you want to be, begin with where you are.

YOUR BUCKET LIST:
CREATE A LIST OF THINGS TO DO BEFORE YOU DIE

So, what are some of the things that you want to do? They might include:

1. Visit Victoria Falls in Africa
2. Visit Robbins Islands in South Africa where Nelson Mandela was incarcerated
3. Shop at Harrods in London, England
4. Climb the Great Wall of China
5. Maintain a positive attitude.
6. Earn your next degree-Associates, Bachelors, Masters or terminal degree.
7. Take a Zumba class
8. Write a bestselling book
9. Take a walk in the shoreline of the Gulf of Mexico.
10. Visit Morocco Africa...to be continued

_____

_____

_____

_____

_____

_____

_____

_____

_____

_____

_____

Be certain that you are not held hostage by doing nothing.

_____/_____/_____
Month   Day   Year

YOUR BUCKET LIST:
CREATE A LIST OF THINGS TO DO BEFORE YOU DIE

THURSDAY:

Be curious.

11. Visit Egypt
12. Visit the Taj Mahal in India
13. Attend a Super Bowl in person
14. Discover your life's passion
15. Run a 5K
16. Run a 10K
17. Discover your priorities. Organize.
18. Run the Peachtree Marathon in Atlanta, GA
19. Run the Boston Marathon
20. Begin to master declarative speech...to be continued

_____

_____

_____

_____

_____

_____

_____

_____

_____

_____

_____

Think about it...there are footprints on the moon, so what is your
reason for not being willing to reach beyond the sky?

YOUR BUCKET LIST:
CREATE A LIST OF THINGS TO DO BEFORE YOU DIE

Just do it.

21. Become fluent in a second language
22. Ride a jet ski
23. Learn to play golf
24. Learn to play tennis
25. Attend the Oscars, Emmys, Grammys and/or Tony Awards
26. Enter a bike race
27. Ride a bicycle from New York to Los Angeles
28. Learn to bowl
29. Learn to play racket ball
30. Learn to play squash
31. Go horseback riding on the beach
32. Heal your past.
33. Learn to ski
34. Ski in the Alps or Vail Colorado
35. Attend the Macy's Thanksgiving Day Parade
36. Stay in the Ice Hotel in Alaska
37. Learn to swim
38. Swim in the ocean
39. Attend the Kentucky Derby
40. Discover what makes you happy...to be continued.

_____

_____

_____

_____

_____

_____

Once the time is gone, it is already gone forever.

_____/_____/_____
Month   Day   Year

YOUR BUCKET LIST:
CREATE A LIST OF THINGS TO DO BEFORE YOU DIE

SATURDAY:

This is your moment and this is your time. Go!

41. Release negative emotions and limiting beliefs
42. Attend or participate in the Summer or Winter Olympics
43. Practice the art of active listening.
44. Go snowboarding
45. Get certified as a lifeguard
46. Get certified in CPR training
47. Learn Judo
48. Go to Times Square and countdown the ball drop for the New Year
49. Ride on a private jet
50. Get a complete makeover...and more.

You get the idea. Now it is time to begin. In life, this is your time. Go!

Action Item: Either start your bucket list or add to it by listing five activities that are far beyond your present 'normal.'

_____

_____

_____

_____

_____

_____

_____

_____

_____

_____

The only person who can stop you is —you!

MEMORABLE MOMENTS

The most memorable moments in life are gems or points of **Reflection** that give you pause. When you place the measuring gauge against your life's journey what moments were the best, worst or those that will go down as the, shall we say, 'teachable moments?'

Action Item: Imagine your box of items designated for safekeeping and list two items that are 'must haves' to be stored there forever.

_____

_____

_____

_____

_____

_____

_____

_____

_____

_____

_____

_____

_____

_____

You can record your dreams, and then,
work to make them come true.

_____/_____/_____
Month   Day   Year

MEMORABLE MOMENTS

MONDAY:

In your box of the best days, would you have the day you received a much better grade than you thought possible, was it graduation day, or the day that you paid off all of your student loans? Was it the day that you met your significant other? Was it your wedding day, the birth of your children, or the birth of your grandchildren?

Reflection: Name the most memorable day of your life.

_____

_____

_____

_____

_____

_____

_____

_____

_____

_____

_____

_____

_____

Embrace your memories and they will give you comfort.

_____/_____/_____
Month   Day   Year

MEMORABLE MOMENTS

TUESDAY:

Would your days of **Reflection** include the loss of a loved one, the regret that you now have because you didn't share your feelings with a person who gave you guidance when you simply did not want to listen or was it when a friend that you thought was true to the end was actually false and self-absorbed.

Action Item: Identify your most challenging misfortune that you had to overcome.

_____

_____

_____

_____

_____

_____

_____

_____

_____

_____

_____

_____

_____

_____

_____

_____

You may not succeed the first time you try...keep trying.

_____/_____/_____
Month   Day   Year

MEMORABLE MOMENTS

WEDNESDAY:

The good news is that there are lessons learned in whatever comes our way. You just have to be wise enough to stay alert and appreciative that you had the chance to be engaged in situations, circumstances and/or to meet people who give you joy or at least a frame of reference for future.

Action Item: List two of your greatest life lessons.

_____

_____

_____

_____

_____

_____

_____

_____

_____

_____

_____

_____

_____

_____

Don't forget... Do something, even if you are moving one step at a time. Just be very sure, that you are not standing still.

MEMORABLE MOMENTS

For sure, life has many special moments. Yes, it is analogous to thinking about a certain song when it comes on the radio. You are writing a card to a friend, and they call at the exact same time that you are writing to them. The best moments and memories are those that are unplanned.

Action Item: Capture your special memories. List two that you shall never forget.

_____

_____

_____

_____

_____

_____

_____

_____

_____

_____

_____

_____

_____

Learn as though you will live forever;
live as though you will die tomorrow.

_____/_____/_____
Month   Day   Year

MEMORABLE MOMENTS

FRIDAY:

Memorable moments are life shaping and character building. Some things will set your life course as to who you will become. At the time, they may seem insignificant or inconsequential, but they really will be important. These moments build who you are and who you will become.

Action Item: Identify the place, time and circumstance when you were the champion of a difficult situation.

_____

_____

_____

_____

_____

_____

_____

_____

_____

_____

_____

_____

_____

Notice that the bigger the challenge, the greater the opportunity.
With growth, you will find measurable change and
self-improvement.

MEMORABLE MOMENTS

SATURDAY:

Remember that there are three things you can never recover in life: the moment after it's gone, the word after it has been spoken, and the time that has already been wasted. Everyday there is an opportunity to savor the moment, and then to enjoy the richness that living life affords. Create the memories that touch you at the heart level.

Action Item: Describe the value of time and how your wise use of it is essential to your well-being.

_____

_____

_____

_____

_____

_____

_____

_____

_____

_____

_____

_____

_____

Don't limit your imagination.

_____/_____/_____
Month   Day   Year

COUSINS

SUNDAY:

It is a family affair, immediate or extended. It is amazing how many times we claim someone else as being our cousin by blood, marriage, or play cousin, because that person was a neighbor's child so they were just a like brother or sister. If dinner was being served, there was always room for them to eat a meal. And, if they got out of line, your parents would discipline them as quickly as they would discipline you.

Action Item: What does family mean to you?

_____

_____

_____

_____

_____

_____

_____

_____

_____

_____

_____

_____

_____

_____

_____

_____

No matter what happened, cousins are always there.

COUSINS

With a burgeoning number of family reunions, sojourns, cruises, weekends planned to shop, take in plays or concerts, or to hunt or fish, families are getting closer. Family members are becoming more inclusive. "Is that your cousin?" "No, that is not my cousin, but, that is my cousin's cousin's cousin, so that is my cousin."

Reflection: Do you have a genuine interest in family or find that you are more comfortable with friends?

_____

_____

_____

_____

_____

_____

_____

_____

_____

_____

_____

_____

_____

_____

Family can easily become comparable to tree limbs
reaching far beyond the original roots.

/   /
Month   Day   Year

COUSINS

TUESDAY:

It turns out that cousins are friends, pals and partners in good and bad times. They hold secrets, better than most, even when everyone wants to know your details. Cousins are there for you in that they are being genuine when they ask how you are doing; they really do want the answer. So they listen.

Reflection: Have your cousins become surrogate siblings?

_____

_____

_____

_____

_____

_____

_____

_____

_____

_____

_____

_____

No one else may know your secret,
but you feel compelled to tell your cousin.

____/____/____
Month   Day   Year

COUSINS

Cousins by blood, friends by choice. A real cousin (or friend) is someone who walks in when the rest of the world walks out. There are levels of cousinship, ranging from first, second and third cousins who can be once or twice removed.

Reflection: Is a blood relationship a banner or a burden?

_____

_____

_____

_____

_____

_____

_____

_____

_____

_____

_____

_____

_____

_____

A cousin sees the first tear,
catches the second and stops the third.

_____/_____/_____
Month   Day   Year

COUSINS

THURSDAY:

When we think of family, we think of glue, or even a stronger substance, cement, that brings us closer together. We understand each other; accept our weaknesses and applaud our strengths.

Action Item: What are two strengths that you have and you attribute to your families' influence?

_____

_____

_____

_____

_____

_____

_____

_____

_____

_____

_____

_____

_____

_____

As cousins, pictures may fade,
but your memories will last forever.

COUSINS

Life is really about family. It is their love, outreach, accommodation, and availability to travel with you on your journey. Remember family helps to make a house a home, not a house standing alone, without the people who make it live, breathe and have its being.

Action Item: List five features of your family that has made your house, your home.

_____

_____

_____

_____

_____

_____

_____

_____

_____

_____

_____

_____

_____

_____

Cousins grow up to be lifetime friends.

_____/_____/_____
Month   Day   Year

COUSINS

SATURDAY:

You can choose your friends, but not your family. Family ties are treasures. Most family members celebrate your victories, empathize with you when you miss the mark, cheer you on to the finish line and reflect with you when life makes you feel as if you will simply melt.

Reflection: Have you been able to find the best in your family members or not?

_____

_____

_____

_____

_____

_____

_____

_____

_____

_____

_____

_____

_____

_____

_____

Family: together, they will.

_____

___/___/___
Month Day Year

58

MEDITATION: SOOTHING SERUM

We live in a busy, busy, society. Typically, we are rushing to just catch up with ourselves. Based upon all that there is to do, we end up wondering everyday how to manage the feat of completing the tasks assigned to our hand.

Reflection: Meditation is the dissolution of thoughts in eternal awareness. It is knowing without thinking.

_____

_____

_____

_____

_____

_____

_____

_____

_____

_____

_____

_____

If another has offended you, seek to raise your spirit so high that the offense cannot reach you.

_____/_____/_____
Month   Day   Year

MEDITATION: SOOTHING SERUM

MONDAY:

To our detriment, it is hard to concentrate. We worry, and try to be all that we are supposed to be. We are worn out, frazzled and engaging in self-criticism, not convinced that the efforts extended matched the desired quality product.

Reflection: We live in a world starved for solitude, silence, and privacy. We are starved for meditation and true friendship.

_____

_____

_____

_____

_____

_____

_____

_____

_____

_____

_____

_____

_____

_____

_____

"Meditation is not a way of making your mind quiet. It's a way of entering into the quiet that's already there—buried under the 50,000 thoughts the average person thinks every day."
– Deepak Chopra

_____/_____/_____
Month   Day   Year

60

MEDITATION: SOOTHING SERUM

TUESDAY:

Life includes anxiety, frustration and worry, negative chatter and stress, but meditation can ease, if not eliminate, those blockers to your peace and quiet. With consistency, your mind will sharpen, and concentration abilities will increase. Having a calm place to go mentally, to get in touch with yourself will assist in responding to everything that is a 'must do' on your agenda.

Reflection: If you wrap your ribbon only around yourself, you have a small package, indeed.

_____

_____

_____

_____

_____

_____

_____

_____

_____

_____

_____

_____

_____

_____

_____

"Meditation brings wisdom and lack of mediation leaves ignorance."
—Buddha

61

_____/_____/_____
Month   Day   Year

MEDITATION: SOOTHING SERUM

WEDNESDAY:

Through meditation, the effort is to stop the racing and rushing of thoughts in your mind. You want to slow down, not only during meditation, but also in daily life. Happiness, tolerance, love, understanding, inner power and fearlessness increase along the way. Meditation is more than relaxation.

Action Item: Describe any personal meditation experience.

_____

_____

_____

_____

_____

_____

_____

_____

_____

_____

_____

_____

_____

_____

_____

"The spirit is something to be enjoyed.
It is not a harsh discipline."
–Shirley MacLaine

MEDITATION: SOOTHING SERUM

Are you in touch with what relaxes you? Is it walking by the beach, reading a book or getting a massage? Think about it, it could be simply breaking your daily routine.

Action Item: What in your life takes you to a place that eases your mind, calms your spirit, and relaxes your body while simultaneously minimizing tension?

_____

_____

_____

_____

_____

_____

_____

_____

_____

_____

_____

_____

_____

_____

Meditation…releases your thoughts. It eases your brain and introduces you to yourself.

_____/_____/_____
Month   Day   Year

63

MEDITATION: SOOTHING SERUM

FRIDAY:

Imagine that you could mentally still away...just for a second. Close your eyes, and enter deep meditation. In a matter of minutes, you are focused, without restlessness or distractions. Pause and do this every day. It is expected that you will get to know yourself better through your personal epiphanies, and become more self-aware. You will be encouraged, inspired, and healthier.

Reflection: If you took a five-minute vacation, where would you visit?

_____

_____

_____

_____

_____

_____

_____

_____

_____

_____

_____

_____

_____

"Empty your mind, be formless, shapeless—like water...
put water into a cup, it becomes the cup...you put it in a teapot,
it becomes the teapot. Be water..."
—Bruce Lee

MEDITATION: SOOTHING SERUM

The value of meditation is not that you go into your private closet and go 'humm.' It is to engage in peaceful introspection away from the noise and activity of the day.

Reflection: Meditation creates more time than it takes.

_____

_____

_____

_____

_____

_____

_____

_____

_____

_____

_____

_____

_____

_____

_____

_____

_____

"Meditation is acceptance."
– Sri Chinmoy

_____

____/____/____
Month Day Year

65

MARCH

Introspection

"The thing that makes you exceptional, if you are at all, is inevitably that which must also make you lonely."
—Lorraine Hansberry

KEEP IT MOVING

It is true, that life happens when you have other plans. Therefore, it is very important that you associate with people who are moving forward. There is not enough time in life either to get mad at others or to get even, instead, you have a responsibility to get busy, and keep it moving. Don't insist upon looking back, because that is not the direction that you are going.

Action Item: Identify two times when your life was appreciably out of sync with your plans. You thought things would go one way and your world was turned upside down.

_____

_____

_____

_____

_____

_____

_____

_____

_____

_____

_____

_____

Use your talents, skills, abilities, expertise to do what you capable of doing, and then, you will shock yourself!

_____/_____/_____
Month   Day   Year

KEEP IT MOVING

MONDAY:

Life is a roller coaster. Things don't always happen just like you have planned. Because, the likelihood that you will be dealing with human beings is quite high, therefore, you must make allowances for their need to veer away from the script. On a roller coaster, you can make a decision to scream every time you hit a bump or you can throw your hands up in the air and simply enjoy!

Action Item: Have you ever just flipped the script in your life and decided to take life as it is? Why?

_____

_____

_____

_____

_____

_____

_____

_____

_____

_____

_____

_____

_____

_____

At times, it is the last key in the box that will unlock the door.

KEEP IT MOVING

Remember that the past is where you learned the lesson. The future is where you apply the lesson. The challenge is to refuse to give up or give out in the middle. When you fall or even fail, and yes, you will do both, it is called life, it is your opportunity to get up and get going.

Action Item: List three life lessons learned that have enriched your life.

_____

_____

_____

_____

_____

_____

_____

_____

_____

_____

_____

_____

_____

Never give up. Never give up, because when you do, you just
may be at the place where the tide will turn.

_____/_____/_____
Month   Day   Year

69

KEEP IT MOVING

WEDNESDAY:

At times, failure is a wakeup call to show you that you must press forward. Prepare. If you get down, don't stay down. Prepare to overcome. Push yourself to the top, or get trampled by those who are en route to the top.

Reflection: Have you ever put your alarm clock on snooze and it worked to your disadvantage?

_____

_____

_____

_____

_____

_____

_____

_____

_____

_____

_____

_____

Don't forget... Evaluate what you become by achieving your
goals, not just the fact that you actually were able to do what you
set out to accomplish.

KEEP IT MOVING

It impresses me that the residents of many of the Caribbean Islands greet you by saying, "Good Day!" It is so pleasant and focused on the best of the day. For me, that greeting cancels the negative and emphasizes the positive. It pushes one to live in the moment and realize that at times, all doors maybe closed, but they aren't locked.

Reflection: Name something in your life that 'rocks' your world!

_____

_____

_____

_____

_____

_____

_____

_____

_____

_____

_____

_____

_____

Always be confident that you can do your best.

/ /
Month   Day   Year

71

KEEP IT MOVING

FRIDAY:

Find a way, because there is one. Life is like riding a bicycle. To keep your balance, you must keep moving. There are more than a few things in life that will make you smile. Find them.

Reflection: Be creative—always. How has your creativity worked to your advantage?

_____

_____

_____

_____

_____

_____

_____

_____

_____

_____

_____

_____

This is a new day —keep it moving!

_____/_____/_____
Month   Day   Year

KEEP IT MOVING

SATURDAY:

Forget all of the reasons why your plans won't work and believe in the one reason why they will, even if no one else believes. It is your life to live. Keep it moving. Life is about going forward no matter what is in front of you.

Reflection: Think about the time when you were your own cheerleader. Others did not believe that you could win, but you did. How did you feel?

_____

_____

_____

_____

_____

_____

_____

_____

_____

_____

_____

_____

_____

_____

Consider this... The only way out...may be...forward.

73

_____/_____/_____
Month   Day   Year

MIRROR, MIRROR ON THE WALL

SUNDAY:

It is important to know who you are. It is in those still, quiet moments of communion with oneself that there is a discovery of thoughts, ideas, issues and concerns, and yes, secrets that have not been shared, otherwise. There is a revealing silence in the heart. Your visions become very clear when you are willing and able to look into your own mind, body and spirit.

Reflection: Prepare...You can run but you really can't hide. The only way out, is in.

_____

_____

_____

_____

_____

_____

_____

_____

_____

_____

_____

_____

_____

_____

"Know thyself."
—Socrates.

MIRROR, MIRROR ON THE WALL

MONDAY:

The process of aging is real and irrefutable. Your next phase of self is always just around the next year. Isn't that special? Be assured, that after all of the lotions, potions, oils, and spa visits, gravity is a master at pulling the body down.

Reflection: Don't lie...your soul knows the truth.

_____

_____

_____

_____

_____

_____

_____

_____

_____

_____

_____

_____

_____

Don't cry because it's over, smile because it happened.

____/____/____
Month   Day   Year

MIRROR, MIRROR ON THE WALL

TUESDAY:

It is true, that as human beings, we are always a 'work in progress,' as opposed to having been complete upon arrival. The only journey is from within. Your image is going to change. So, the real question is what is your life's purpose as you master new skills?

Reflection: Don't forget...Life will never be perfect. Step outside of yourself and consider your own shortcomings.

_____

_____

_____

_____

_____

_____

_____

_____

_____

_____

_____

_____

Before you assume, learn. Before you judge, understand.
Before you hurt, feel. Before you say, think.

MIRROR, MIRROR ON THE WALL

We are empowered to look beyond our outside appearance to the true person within. The U.S. Census Bureau announced that, within 10 years and for the first time in history, old people will outnumber young people across the globe. These facts are encouraging.

Reflection: Seek to know who you are and how you are, even if you have to visit some dark corners.

_____

_____

_____

_____

_____

_____

_____

_____

_____

_____

_____

_____

_____

_____

_____

Nothing is really work unless you would rather be doing something else.

_____/_____/_____
Month   Day   Year

MIRROR, MIRROR ON THE WALL

Thursday:

THURSDAY:

Seasoned individuals are inclined to let their curiosity encourage them to try something new. They have time to explore and discover new things ranging from art and culture.

Reflection: Introspection...has no end.

_____

_____

_____

_____

_____

_____

_____

_____

_____

_____

_____

_____

_____

_____

_____

_____

*"Sometimes the questions are complicated
and the answers are simple."*
–Dr. Seuss

____/____/_____
Month   Day   Year

MIRROR, MIRROR ON THE WALL

FRIDAY:

The nation is on the move. The citizenry has decided to get involved with doing something with their mind and body to improve their spirit. So, they are stretching, exercising and improving their strength and flexibility.

Reflection: Keep trying, hold on, and always, believe in yourself, because if you don't, then who will?

_____

_____

_____

_____

_____

_____

_____

_____

_____

_____

_____

"Finish each day and be done with it...Some blunders and
absurdities no doubt crept in; forget them as soon as you can.
Tomorrow is a new day... begin it serenely...without nonsense."
–Ralph Waldo Emerson

_____/_____/_____
Month   Day   Year

MIRROR, MIRROR ON THE WALL

SATURDAY:

Alleviate stress; improve your mood. What you believe is your decision. But, be certain that you realize that you don't have all the answers. Consistently seek to find comfort in the study and knowledge of your beliefs.

Reflection: If you are bored with life, you don't have enough to do.

_____

_____

_____

_____

_____

_____

_____

_____

_____

_____

_____

_____

_____

_____

I may not have gone where I intended to go,
but I think I have ended up where I needed to be.

_____/_____/_____
Month   Day   Year

LESS IS MORE

"Don't use a lot where a little will do." -Proverb

Reflection: Being frugal has advantages.

_____

_____

_____

_____

_____

_____

_____

_____

_____

_____

_____

_____

_____

_____

If something is frustrating you, simplify it.

_____/_____/_____
Month Day Year

LESS IS MORE

MONDAY:

In many instances, the society has gone mad in search of itself. There are those who mistakenly think they can indulge in larger portions of food, just because it is served; use more make-up, because they think it is fashionable; or talk and keep talking while others are listening. Again, take a hint. Less is more.

Reflection: How do you think our society arrived at dealing in excesses?

_____

_____

_____

_____

_____

_____

_____

_____

_____

_____

_____

_____

_____

_____

_____

_____

Take responsibility for the way that you behave.

LESS IS MORE

Notwithstanding your vision, the mindset that less is more can be an important concept for your positive consideration. Set your priorities. Organize. Identify your resources. You need to decide to make life better by being more specific and more deliberate.

Action Item: Name two of your most valuable resources.

_____

_____

_____

_____

_____

_____

_____

_____

_____

_____

_____

_____

Forgiveness will make you wealthy.
It keeps you from being robbed by anger, excesses,
and changing the way you handle things.

_____/_____/_____
Month   Day   Year

LESS IS MORE

If you live your life trying to impress people, your life is going to be complicated. If you don't want to be around a certain group of friends, do not invite them to an event. Do what enriches your spirit, rather than engage in activities that you are doing just...because.

Reflection: Do you have a formula for selecting your friends?

_____

_____

_____

_____

_____

_____

_____

_____

_____

_____

_____

_____

_____

_____

_____

Make up your mind that you are going to enjoy life.

_____/_____/_____
Month   Day   Year

LESS IS MORE

A physician shared that while on a seven-day cruise she was thrilled to have her cell phone turned off. No paging, no status checks, no answering service reports. Instead, it was simply a much-needed vacation.

Reflection: Take time and give attention to yourself. You are the only you that you have.

_____

_____

_____

_____

_____

_____

_____

_____

_____

_____

_____

_____

_____

_____

_____

_____

Keep it simple.

____/____/____
Month Day Year

LESS IS MORE

FRIDAY:

Think about how easy it is to eat a whole bag of chips, or a can of nuts or a bowl of ice cream. At the time, they all seem bottomless. So, you continue to indulge until you have eaten 'the whole thing.' When things are readily accessible, internet and television for example, perhaps you should go to another room, and engage your time in a more efficient and effective activity.

Reflection: Think about wasting time and talent on being self-serving versus being productive.

_____

_____

_____

_____

_____

_____

_____

_____

_____

_____

_____

_____

_____

Don't complicate things. Don't overdo.

_____/_____/_____
Month Day Year

LESS IS MORE

Those who are technologically savvy, easily send not only thank you, or anniversary or birthday cards by email; the send button has replaced the post office. Take another step. Select either a blank or an all occasion card and send one to family or friends. Your simple act of kindness will make their day.

Action Item: Do something personal for another person.

_____

_____

_____

_____

_____

_____

_____

_____

_____

_____

_____

_____

Do this for yourself. Seek peace and happiness.

_____/_____/_____
Month   Day   Year

PEER POWER

Research reveals in early childhood, as early as six months old, when viewing photographs of people struggling up a hill, a preference was shown for those who help, not hinder. Peer power can make a critical difference in what you do, how you do it and how you are viewed and/or accepted by others.

Action Item: People favor top dogs, but they fight for under dogs. Have you ever fought for an underdog? What was the result? How did you feel?

_____

_____

_____

_____

_____

_____

_____

_____

_____

_____

_____

_____

_____

_____

*There is some good in the worst of us and some bad in the
best of us – and you don't have a monopoly on either.*

_____/_____/_____
Month Day   Year

PEER POWER

Don't let anyone rain on your parade. You can be inclusive, without being controlled by others. A peer group can keep you confident, encourage you to solve problems, engage in decision-making and negate hidden agendas.

Action Item: You are your own responsibility. Give two examples of 'creating your own sunshine.'

_____

_____

_____

_____

_____

_____

_____

_____

_____

_____

_____

_____

If you are not a change agent,
change will overtake and possible overturn you.

89

_____/_____/_____
Month   Day   Year

PEER POWER

TUESDAY:

True influence includes good character, integrity, leadership, trust and transparency, not domination or control.

Action Item: List three quality characteristics of your personality that are assets. List three characteristics that you know you need to change.

_____

_____

_____

_____

_____

_____

_____

_____

_____

_____

_____

_____

_____

_____

_____

You have the power to set the example.
Always be more willing to give than to receive.

PEER POWER

WEDNESDAY:

It is important to seek and find like-minded people to assist you in being your best. We learn from each other in the discovery of becoming our best self.

Action Item: Name three of your best friends and identify how they make you grow.

_____

_____

_____

_____

_____

_____

_____

_____

_____

_____

_____

_____

You can control your friend circle or you can let someone else control your destiny.

_____/_____/_____
Month Day   Year

91

PEER POWER

It is ill-advised to seek power for power's sake. Fear is not the controlling element. Be clear, warriors take chances. Set your own goals and objectives so that you always seek to reach the standards that you have set for yourself.

Action Item: Decide what two things are worth the risk to improve your professional growth and development.

_____

_____

_____

_____

_____

_____

_____

_____

_____

_____

_____

_____

_____

_____

_____

_____

To demonstrate real power, first you must master yourself.

PEER POWER

Yours is not to imitate or emulate. Avoid jealousy, anger or greed. The real benefit comes when you are determined to seek power to do the right thing with and for those who will benefit from your selfless actions.

Action Item: Measure your strengths, and decide on four that are your strongest attributes, and why?

_____

_____

_____

_____

_____

_____

_____

_____

_____

_____

_____

_____

_____

Be certain to control your life. You have only one life to live.

_____/_____/_____
Month   Day   Year

PEER POWER

Have principles, values and beliefs of your own. The core of your being is your attitude toward others and therefore, toward, yourself. You are command central, waiting for your instructions.

Reflection: You are in charge of your destiny. Yes, the captain of your ship. Are you steering in the right direction?

_____

_____

_____

_____

_____

_____

_____

_____

_____

_____

_____

_____

_____

_____

*Understand that...a person's thoughts and actions are
inextricably bound one to the other.*

____/____/_____
Month   Day   Year

April

Change

"If you don't like something, change it; if you can't change it,
change the way you think about it."
—Mary Engelbreit

MONDAY IS COMING!

SUNDAY:

Depend on it, you will not wake up and hear the news report that Monday has been cancelled and you can go back to sleep. Experts report that often one's workplace production is a mere 13% on Monday. However, Monday is the key day of the workweek. You want to begin with the end in mind.

Action Item: What is the greatest day of workplace productivity?

_____

_____

_____

_____

_____

_____

_____

_____

_____

_____

_____

_____

*Are you self-serving…waiting…after inquiring from others or
are you anxious to share your own story?*

MONDAY IS COMING!

MONDAY:

Of course, everyone has the opportunity of dealing with Mondays that are deemed to be holidays. In doing so, we can enjoy a long weekend.

Action Item: Identify your favorite holiday and why?

_____

_____

_____

_____

_____

_____

_____

_____

_____

_____

_____

_____

_____

_____

_____

Do something on Monday other than start a new diet.

_____/_____/_____
Month   Day   Year

MONDAY IS COMING!

TUESDAY:

On some Mondays, mail is neither picked up nor delivered. Retail store hours are often altered. And, if you don't have access to more than one television in your home, you may be relegated to watching on-going sports games with some type of competitive sport, which includes a round, oblong, large or small ball. You are right-baseball, basketball, or football. Isn't that special?

Action Item: What activity is best accomplished on Monday?

_____

_____

_____

_____

_____

_____

_____

_____

_____

_____

_____

_____

_____

Compare middle age to a long weekend on Monday afternoon.

MONDAY IS COMING!

Circumstances cannot always be changed. But, the fact still remains, whatever there is to be changed, it must first be faced. There is value in looking at Monday as a day of productivity, a day of doing something that matters, and a day that will make a meaningful difference.

Action Item: What project do you find that you have been putting off to 'every Monday?'

_____

_____

_____

_____

_____

_____

_____

_____

_____

_____

_____

_____

_____

_____

_____

_____

_____

_____

_____

_____

_____

_____

_____

_____

_____

Think about it. A weekend wasted is not a wasted weekend.

_____

99

_____/_____/_____
Month   Day   Year

MONDAY IS COMING!

THURSDAY:

Keep your eye on the goal and you mind focused on the fact that every Monday you have a fresh chance to renew your plan for betterment.

Action Item: What can you do on Monday that enhances your life, family or community?

_____

_____

_____

_____

_____

_____

_____

_____

_____

_____

_____

_____

_____

_____

Good advice: Look forward to going to work on Monday.
Some people don't have a job to go to.

___/___/___
Month Day Year

MONDAY IS COMING!

Figure out challenges that seem impossible to overcome. You have the talent to address the problem. Find a solution. The greatest inspiration is often born of desperation. It has been rightly stated, that things turn out best for those who make the best of the way things turn out.

Reflection: Identify how you solved your greatest life challenge within the last five years.

_____

_____

_____

_____

_____

_____

_____

_____

_____

_____

_____

_____

_____

_____

_____

Ask yourself, whether there are enough days in the weekend?

_____

_____/_____/_____
Month   Day   Year

MONDAY IS COMING!

SATURDAY:

A holiday, Monday has become the blockbuster day for holidays, retail sales, backyard barbecues and an effort to 'catch up' on all of those yesterdays. Pause and refuel. Every week you also have Friday through Sunday. Take advantage.

Action Item: How do you renew, refuel and refresh?

_____

_____

_____

_____

_____

_____

_____

_____

_____

_____

_____

_____

_____

_____

Think about it...if you cook once, it should feed you twice.

CHANGE: THE INCONVENIENT TRUTH

We have become set in our ways, comfortable and satisfied, because we stick like glue to the things that we know, the people that we enjoy, and the places that we frequent. We become non-adventuresome, inflexible, and framed by the portrait that we know to be ourselves.

Action Item: Give two examples of major changes that you have made to adjust to be a change agent and resulting benefit(s).

_____

_____

_____

_____

_____

_____

_____

_____

_____

_____

_____

_____

_____

_____

Prepare...a change for betterment, lies within you.

_____/_____/_____
Month   Day   Year

CHANGE: THE INCONVENIENT TRUTH

MONDAY:

Change can be disruptive, and shocking. The way things were, are not the way they are or will be. In other words, the 'good old days' are gone, and won't be back. Be prepared or prepare to be swept away. Remain convinced that you are equal to the challenge, and can survive it.

Action Item: Imagine a storm warning that has been given and the need to 'prepare.' What action would you take? Why?

_____

_____

_____

_____

_____

_____

_____

_____

_____

_____

_____

_____

_____

_____

Even a change for the better has some discomforts.

CHANGE: THE INCONVENIENT TRUTH

'The only constant is change itself.' Change is everywhere. Refuse to lament about what used to be. In the midst of mixed signals, ambiguous rules and directions, traditions and habits are being moved out of the way in favor of new ones. Data and information are power. Prioritize your specialized knowledge and skill sets.

Action Item: List five professional skills that are in your toolbox to make yourself ready for today's workplace.

_____

_____

_____

_____

_____

_____

_____

_____

_____

_____

_____

_____

The future comes, one day at a time.

_____/_____/_____
Month   Day   Year

CHANGE: THE INCONVENIENT TRUTH

WEDNESDAY:

Be certain that you don't take yourself too seriously. Remember, working together works, and you never know with whom you will have to work whether in your household, at work or in an organization in an effort to contribute. Be a positive change agent, rather than an individual who cannot adjust or adapt to endure.

Reflection: What is meant by the statement: "Be excellent, but keep your nose at a friendly level?"

_____

_____

_____

_____

_____

_____

_____

_____

_____

_____

_____

_____

_____

We want to leave behind a bit of our best selves.

CHANGE: THE INCONVENIENT TRUTH

THURSDAY:

Tell the truth, how well do you get along with your colleagues or peers? Perhaps you see yourself in the best light; and you may also decide that you are a better leader, manager, career professional or student than those with whom you are working. If there is a problem, a concern, or an issue, you may decide that the difficulty lies with the other person. Isn't that special?

Action Item: List three of your strengths and weaknesses. You have some of both.

_____

_____

_____

_____

_____

_____

_____

_____

_____

_____

_____

_____

_____

_____

_____

We are the ones that we have been waiting for.

107

___/___/___
Month Day Year

CHANGE: THE INCONVENIENT TRUTH

FRIDAY:

Ask yourself, "How can I improve in my decision making, communication, personal and professional development, sooner, rather than later?" Be a champion of change. Have a plan and work your plan for meeting your goals in your one-year, five year, ten-year plan. Decide what you want to do. Share your aspirations with others who can benefit you.

Reflection: To reach your destination, how will you begin?

_____

_____

_____

_____

_____

_____

_____

_____

_____

_____

_____

_____

_____

_____

_____

_____

Forward ever, backward never.

_____/_____/_____
Month   Day   Year

CHANGE: THE INCONVENIENT TRUTH

SATURDAY:

Ambitious people get noticed. Be wise. Demonstrate flexibility, open-mindedness, a strong work ethic and a focus on the future. Use those qualities for this dynamic period.

Action Item: Share your goals and timetables for your professional growth and development. Has there been a change? If so, why?

_____

_____

_____

_____

_____

_____

_____

_____

_____

_____

_____

_____

_____

Action and reaction, ebb and flow, trial and error...
change is the rhythm of living.

_____ / _____ / _____
Month   Day   Year

109

THE NEW NORMAL

SUNDAY:

Doesn't it always seem that the moment you think that you have today's terminology down to a science, it changes? Now, the old way of doing things, has changed. Yes, that which was, shall we say, routine, has evolved into a 21st century 'new normal.'

Action Item: List three distinctly different realties of the 'new normal.'

_____

_____

_____

_____

_____

_____

_____

_____

_____

_____

_____

_____

_____

_____

Normal is subjective. In our society,
a perfectly normal situation is rare.

THE NEW NORMAL

The policies, practices and procedures are new and different. They are also unforgiving. It is clear that problem solving will be required. Either you know or you don't. You will be competitive or not. You will need to be in the swing of things or you don't have to be. Where you are or are not depends on you.

Action Item: What side of the aisle are you traveling on the road to the possible? Explain.

_____

_____

_____

_____

_____

_____

_____

_____

_____

_____

_____

_____

_____

Normal is an idea. But, it is not reality. Reality is brutal,
but with persistence, it can turn nothing into something.

____/____/____
Month Day Year

THE NEW NORMAL

TUESDAY:

Collectively, our concerns are far reaching. They are neither isolated nor do they afford you the opportunity to insulate yourself from being the adult who takes charge and engages in decisive action.

Reflection: Describe what it means to you to be bold and courageous versus being reticent in your decision-making.

_____

_____

_____

_____

_____

_____

_____

_____

_____

_____

_____

_____

_____

_____

Refuse mere normalcy. Embrace your potential.

_____/_____/_____
Month   Day   Year

THE NEW NORMAL

WEDNESDAY:

Those who have always managed, understood, strategically planned and expertly executed, become unsure. Necessarily, you ask, "when that which we know to be true, is no more, what does the 'new normal' look like?"

Action Item: Project to five and ten years from now, and list two new, different and significant changes that you think will be a part of everyday life.

_____

_____

_____

_____

_____

_____

_____

_____

_____

_____

_____

_____

_____

_____

*That which was normal has been replaced or
altered by the new and improved.*

_____/_____/_____
Month   Day   Year

THE NEW NORMAL

THURSDAY:

We want to know how we will survive in the midst of a plethora of problems, including, economic concerns, ecological impact issues, scarcity and the list continues. In planning and execution, we have also learned that bigger is not always better.

Action Item: Identify your single most pressing challenge. List two reasons why.

_____

_____

_____

_____

_____

_____

_____

_____

_____

_____

_____

_____

_____

_____

Know when to hold, when to fold, and when to walk away.

_____/_____/_____
Month   Day   Year

THE NEW NORMAL

The clarion call is to utilize vision, courage and effort to have a sustainable life. Our goal is to find answers in business, science, finance, politics, and education.

Refection: In a self-assessment, do you think that you are a dedicated visionary, steadily working on solutions, rather than complaining about problems?

_____

_____

_____

_____

_____

_____

_____

_____

_____

_____

_____

_____

_____

A normal state of things can be boring.
Go for the vibrancy of change.

115

THE NEW NORMAL

The Internet is rapidly enhancing the very nature of communication, including the evolution of opinion and advocacy. We seek new motivators to find a new normal that is secure, stable and sensible. As a society, we are in the fast forward lane. The real question is do we, as drivers, know whether and when to put on the brakes?

Action Item: List five tasks that were difficult and different which at first you thought were out of your realm. What lessons learned were common to each task?

_____

_____

_____

_____

_____

_____

_____

_____

_____

_____

_____

_____

_____

Direct your compass toward love, hope, compassion and courage.
Decide what is normal for you.

A MICROWAVE SOCIETY

There is a new mindset in this society. We want 'it' now, whatever the 'it' is. Today we have a host of conveniences, and expect more. There is no time to wait. Therefore, everyone and everything is on speed dial. The angst expressed over "What took so long?" actually causes great debates.

Action Item: Does haste make waste in your life? List three examples.

_____

_____

_____

_____

_____

_____

_____

_____

_____

_____

_____

_____

_____

_____

_____

Remember there is real value in using a crock-pot,
not a microwave.

_____/_____/_____
Month   Day   Year

A MICROWAVE SOCIETY

MONDAY:

Have you prepared a full meal in less than thirty minutes; or, are you a student who can't understand that it will take at least a three-day weekend for the professor to post the final grades; or, have absolute frustration when SKYPE fails to provide an automatic connection. We want it all in record time.

Action Item: List two examples of having to wait and explain how you handled your dissatisfaction.

_____

_____

_____

_____

_____

_____

_____

_____

_____

_____

_____

_____

_____

_____

_____

Time is silent and without limits.

A MICROWAVE SOCIETY

TUESDAY:

Everything is fast and easy. There is a disregard for good, wholesome nutrition, exercise, the requisite amount of sleep, quality deliverables at work, school or community. There simply isn't time or so we think. Both individuals and families take the hit. And, relationships don't always bounce back for a second chance.

Reflection: Think about a time in your life that may have been different if you had taken/given more time.

_____

_____

_____

_____

_____

_____

_____

_____

_____

_____

_____

_____

A lifetime isn't forever, so take the first chance,
don't wait for the second one!

_____/_____/_____
Month   Day   Year

A MICROWAVE SOCIETY

WEDNESDAY:

Our challenges today are legion. We want prosperity, health, success and happiness, as a package deal. However, we often do not have the required sacrifice, work, and patience. The established agenda is instantaneous. No shortcuts or compromises.

Action Item: List five things that bring value to your life that may not be immediate.

_____

_____

_____

_____

_____

_____

_____

_____

_____

_____

_____

_____

_____

_____

Time is a dressmaker specializing in alterations.

A MICROWAVE SOCIETY

Time itself is the control that keeps everything from happening at once. Time will take care of itself.

Reflection: Life presents its' own next steps, pace and circumstances. Have you experienced superseding intervening causes that have altered or interrupted your plans?

_____

_____

_____

_____

_____

_____

_____

_____

_____

_____

_____

_____

_____

Time is a thief and gives no justice.

_____/_____/_____
Month   Day   Year

A MICROWAVE SOCIETY

FRIDAY:

The message is to slow down. Develop and maintain golden days. Create some memories. Some will come over time as opposed to being 'sensed' in a microwave. Ask yourself, after eight hours of work, and eight hours at home, what else are you doing with your time?

Action Item: If you were unwilling to rush your life, name three things that you would most enjoy that would break your present routine.

_____

_____

_____

_____

_____

_____

_____

_____

_____

_____

_____

_____

_____

If you are willing to learn, time can be a great teacher.

A MICROWAVE SOCIETY

Time is a measurement and still manages to be neither a friend nor an enemy. At the end of the day, you can accept the fact that time does march on. The expectation is that you will use your time wisely. You don't have control over the fact that each day will come and go. Therefore, make sure that your time actually counts.

Reflection: Can you give yourself a 'pat on the back' for how you use your time. Do you have any regrets?

_____

_____

_____

_____

_____

_____

_____

_____

_____

_____

_____

_____

_____

If you want to ensure an exceptional job, select a busy person to do it. Any other person will simply not have the time.

_____/_____/_____
Month   Day   Year

123

May

Education

"The whole world opened to me when I learned to read."
—Mary McLeod Bethune

EDUCATION: THE SECRET

In 1996, everyone wanted to know 'the secret.' They thought it would be life changing, and give them the way to win power, fame, plus the skills that they felt they previously lacked. En masse, people were reading, going to retreats, forums and self-help workshops, to improve themselves.

Reflection: Are your 'secrets' holding you back? Let go and go forward.

_____

_____

_____

Be certain that you are not holding yourself back.

____/____/____
Month   Day   Year

EDUCATION: THE SECRET

MONDAY:

So what is a secret? A secret is that which is kept from knowledge or view: marked by the habit of discretion. It is to be closemouthed, undercover, private, hush-hush, concealed, or undisclosed.

Reflection: Is it possible that you were not to stay here; you are supposed to start here?

_____

_____

_____

_____

_____

_____

_____

_____

_____

_____

_____

_____

_____

Education is the fundamental secret of success. Spread the word.

EDUCATION: THE SECRET

The secret of education is not a message written in secret code for access or completion, no password is required. Instead, education can move those with limitations to limitless horizons.

Reflection: The world is much larger than your comfort zone.

_____

_____

_____

_____

_____

_____

_____

_____

_____

_____

_____

_____

_____

_____

Be willing to try new things.
Securing an education is challenging, but so is life.

_____/_____/_____
Month   Day   Year

EDUCATION: THE SECRET

WEDNESDAY:

To be successful, you have to be prepared to use a result driven action plan. You must take major steps to accomplish the possible for yourself.

Reflection: Success does not include a lackadaisical attitude or laying in your excuses.

_____
_____
_____
_____
_____
_____
_____
_____
_____
_____
_____
_____
_____
_____

Try things that you always wanted to do and see what happens.

EDUCATION: THE SECRET

Your desire may be uncommon, even unusual, but not a secret. There are no silver bullets, panaceas, or magical solutions. You must have a dedicated mind and be prepared for hard work in achieving your education.

Reflection: There are no quick fixes.

_____

_____

_____

_____

_____

_____

_____

_____

_____

_____

_____

_____

_____

_____

_____

*Take advantage of your educational pursuit and all
opportunities that result because of your achievement.*

_____/_____/_____
Month   Day   Year

EDUCATION: THE SECRET

FRIDAY:

Simply put, education requires engagement. Curriculum mastery of literacy, mathematics, technology, the humanities and more, will be significant for your tool kit.

Reflection: Become changed for your own good, notwithstanding those who refuse to be your cheerleader.

_____

_____

_____

_____

_____

_____

_____

_____

_____

_____

_____

_____

Refuse to sit around and do nothing.

EDUCATION: THE SECRET

Don't hold yourself back. Timing is very important. Don't over think the 'whether and when' question. Education is not an option. Shhhhhhh... you know the secret.

Reflection: Know enough that you also know that once you get started, you can't go back.

_____

_____

_____

_____

_____

_____

_____

_____

_____

_____

_____

_____

_____

Education is the best security for age.
Make an assessment of things that have worked for you.

_____/_____/_____
Month   Day   Year

REMEMBER WHEN

It is very hard to explain time. We try to explain it, measure it, classify it, codify it, and recall where the time has possibly gone. Time passes and it waits for no one. While many are getting ready to get ready, time simply, marches on.

Reflection: Believe that tomorrow will be better; and hold on to that thought.

_____

_____

_____

_____

_____

_____

_____

_____

_____

_____

_____

_____

Remember when Mom, Mother, Mamma or
Mud Dear was your only hero?

_____/_____/_____
Month   Day   Year

REMEMBER WHEN

Basically, we are born young, wet, and hungry. Then, you cry, and life is at your door. Remember when you grew up knowing what your parents wanted you to do, and you had to act accordingly? Then, by high school, you were coming into your own, forming your opinions, and thinking that you had most, if not all, of the answers.

Action Item: Time does not wait. What is the greatest memory in your life?

_____

_____

_____

_____

_____

_____

_____

_____

_____

_____

_____

_____

Remember when the worst thing that someone could give you was a cold.

___/___/___
Month   Day   Year

REMEMBER WHEN

Tuesday:

TUESDAY:

Remember when you got the great shock in school that even though you did not work as hard as you could have, you knew that you would get a good grade, and you didn't? Imagine that.

Reflection: Without winter, the spring would not be so refreshing; without adversity, prosperity would not be so rewarding.

_____

_____

_____

_____

_____

_____

_____

_____

_____

_____

_____

_____

_____

_____

*Remember when the worst thing that could hurt you
was skinned knees.*

___/___/_____
Month   Day   Year

REMEMBER WHEN

WEDNESDAY:

Remember when you discovered that those people who are moving forward in the fast lane, rarely wake up and put the alarm clock on snooze? Those who were dedicated and determined to achieve, most often do just that.

Reflection: LIVE your life in such a way that at the end, even the undertaker will be sorry.

Don't let success go to your head.
When success comes, walk in humility.

_____ / _____ / _____
Month   Day   Year

REMEMBER WHEN

THURSDAY:

Remember when you were engaged in a vocabulary adventure as those who were categorized as being poor, then you moved them to the next classification of being needy, deprived, under privileged to disadvantaged. Against the odds, many achieved, while the privileged did not.

Reflection Item: Give to those who have less than you do.

_____

_____

_____

_____

_____

_____

_____

_____

_____

_____

_____

_____

_____

_____

_____

Do the right thing, and few remember.
Do the wrong thing, and no one forgets.

REMEMBER WHEN

Remember when you thought it was just a phrase that "Acts have consequences?" Please know that there is real truth to the saying. Rarely is the perpetrator prepared to handle life's circumstances and situations. Things in life make a full circle.

Reflection: Be certain that you don't take life too seriously. Nobody will escape life—alive.

_____

_____

_____

_____

_____

_____

_____

_____

_____

_____

_____

_____

_____

Remember when 'Goodbye' only meant until tomorrow?

_____ / _____ / _____
Month   Day   Year

REMEMBER WHEN

SATURDAY:

A decision to waste time is not the best decision that you could make. Remember do not regret the process of aging. Not everyone is granted the privilege.

Reflection: Think about it...have you ever stopped to think, and then you forgot to start over again?

_____

_____

_____

_____

_____

_____

_____

_____

_____

_____

_____

_____

_____

_____

*Twenty years from now don't recite a litany of things that you
wish you could have or should have done. Create a juicy past.*

_____/_____/_____
Month   Day   Year

138

EDUCATION:
The Tassel Is Worth The Hassle

Pursue your calling because each one of us has only one life to live. Always be a version of yourself, and not a second version of anybody else. Education is the best provision for old age. Eliminate roadblocks and detours. Opportunities increase as they are seized. Obstacles occur when you take your eyes off your goal.

Action Item: What are the three greatest causes that keep you from reaching your goals?

_____

_____

_____

_____

_____

_____

_____

_____

_____

_____

_____

_____

_____

*The more you learn, the more you should realize
what you do not know.*

_____/_____/_____
Month   Day   Year

139

EDUCATION:
THE TASSEL IS WORTH THE HASSLE

MONDAY:

Education is not an idea to ignore, to put on the back burner or to conclude that you will get around to it—eventually. Access to a quality education has never been easier. The availability of securing an education, curriculum, and the convenience of traditional matriculation or the ease of on-line study. Seek it.

Action Item: What are the benefits of continuing education in your career? List four reasons.

_____

_____

_____

_____

_____

_____

_____

_____

_____

_____

_____

_____

_____

_____

_____

_____

Tomorrow belongs to the people who prepare for it today.

EDUCATION:
THE TASSEL IS WORTH THE HASSLE

Education is a choice that is influenced by many factors, i.e., family circumstances, tuition costs, role models, income levels, and certain social and economic assumptions. Time moves on, and time expects you to be and to remain informed, competitive and current.

Action Item: Name the greatest benefit of securing your education. Name the greatest detriment, if any.

_____

_____

_____

_____

_____

_____

_____

_____

_____

_____

_____

_____

_____

_____

_____

When you educate a woman, you educate a generation.

____/____/____
Month Day Year

EDUCATION:
The Tassel Is Worth The Hassle

WEDNESDAY:

Excellence is an attitude that a dedicated mind can master. In your educational pursuit, there will be red lights, hazards and potholes. You must be willing to go the extra mile and exceed what others are willing to do. En route, it is not whether you get knocked down; it is whether you get up. Victory belongs to the victor.

Reflection: Education allows you to reach for the unthinkable and accomplish the impossible. What is your personal example?

_____

_____

_____

_____

_____

_____

_____

_____

_____

_____

_____

_____

_____

_____

No one can go back and make a brand new start; but you can
start from now and make a brand new ending.

EDUCATION:
The Tassel Is Worth The Hassle

Always be in the 'ready, set, go posture.' There is an ever-present question as to what you plan to do with the rest of your life. Otherwise, you will join the group of those who don't know and don't know that they don't know.

Reflection: Describe the value of your education. List two life-changing differences you have experienced because of your education.

_____

_____

_____

_____

_____

_____

_____

_____

_____

_____

_____

_____

_____

_____

Don't pretend ...there is a real difference between the educated
and the uneducated.

_____/_____/_____
Month   Day   Year

EDUCATION:
The Tassel Is Worth The Hassle

FRIDAY:

It is critical that education serve as a primary component in shaping the values of America's future investments in higher education while producing adults with healthier lives. Education assists your children in being more prepared for school; have lifelong financial benefits at both individual and societal levels; health insurance and pension benefits from their employers, or become self-employed.

Action Item: List four reasons how the lack of education can/will reduce your options in life.

_____

_____

_____

_____

_____

_____

_____

_____

_____

_____

_____

_____

_____

_____

Life is a continuum. When you accomplish one goal, start another. It keeps you from standing still.

___/___/___
Month Day Year

144

EDUCATION:
The Tassel Is Worth The Hassle

It is true; the tassel is worth the hassle. Education pays.

Action Item: List three sacrifices that you made to gain your education. What is your statement regarding your sacrifice, and struggle to achieve your education?

_____

_____

_____

_____

_____

_____

_____

_____

_____

_____

_____

_____

_____

_____

_____

_____

Once a mind is enlightened, it cannot return to darkness.

_____

_____/_____/_____
Month   Day   Year

145

GOOD TO GREAT

Sunday:

SUNDAY:

At the core, we all want to be better. There is a desired pursuit of passion and purpose. Moving from good to great is not a magical occurrence. Instead, it is hard work coupled with a tenacious spirit that is companioned by a doable action plan.

Reflection: Classify your life stage as good, great, extraordinary or world class. Why?

_____

_____

_____

_____

_____

_____

_____

_____

_____

_____

_____

_____

With established goals,
an ordinary person can become extraordinary.

GOOD TO GREAT

At times, something appears to hold you back from being the best, and becoming a significant force of one. Get out of your own way and prepare yourself for success by thinking, feeling, and doing what you know is within, or even beyond your capacity.

Action Item: Identify a significant time when you blocked yourself.

_____

_____

_____

_____

_____

_____

_____

_____

_____

_____

_____

_____

_____

_____

Believe that you can and you will.

_____/_____/_____
Month   Day   Year

147

GOOD TO GREAT

TUESDAY:

Think the thoughts that serve you, feel the feelings that empower you, and do what you know needs to be done. Disciplined thinking combined with disciplined action is an unstoppable force, and it is yours for the taking.

Reflection: Self-discipline is an asset. How have you demonstrated it in your life?

_____

_____

_____

_____

_____

_____

_____

_____

_____

_____

_____

_____

_____

Those who excel in what they do, make decisions, learn and remain committed. Don't give up and don't give in. Be the best.

GOOD TO GREAT

While you look at the models of others who have succeeded, decide how they made it. They did not walk on a red carpet. Each one figured it out that— they would need to visualize, study, evaluate and capture the example set by others, whether in school, business, politics, athletics or entertainment.

Action Item: Give two examples of individuals whom you admired. Why?

_____

_____

_____

_____

_____

_____

_____

_____

_____

_____

_____

_____

_____

_____

_____

It is much easier to become great than to remain great.

_____/_____/_____
Month   Day   Year

GOOD TO GREAT

THURSDAY:

Listen and learn. Sometimes the answers begin by starting backwards. You work your way forward by studying others. Success doesn't just happen; there are clues.

Action Item: Identify three clues that will move you forward, if you take the time to be observant.

_____

_____

_____

_____

_____

_____

_____

_____

_____

_____

_____

_____

_____

Keep going if you intend to reach the next great moment.

GOOD TO GREAT

Collect all your attributes and then bring your best to the table. Know what you can do and what you can't. You can't do everything, but be the best at what you can do. Discover where and when you shine and then go for it.

Action Item: List three things that will give you giant steps forward. Are you following your own schedule? Is it passive or aggressive?

_____

_____

_____

_____

_____

_____

_____

_____

_____

_____

_____

_____

_____

If you want to move forward...move forward. Yesterday's agenda can be viewed as baggage. It is too heavy to carry.

_____/_____/_____
Month   Day   Year

GOOD TO GREAT

SATURDAY:

With thought, you can discover your best. You may need to take tests, be exposed to different career endeavors or activities, before you really know for certain. At first, you will be stunned that you are doing something different. Soon your success will become your signature. Be faithful to your choice, loyal to your desire and convinced that you can be a better you.

Action Item: Write a letter of congratulations to yourself. Job well done.

Critics will always be in place.

NEXT STEPS:
BE A THOUGHT LEADER

It's a truism that thought leaders tend to be the most successful individuals in their respective fields. If you want to be in the spotlight, and to be known as a person who using a telescope in shaping their thoughts and ideas, then become a thought leader. Researchers agree that being a thought leader, whether you're an individual or employed at an organization, you are a possibility thinker who embraces the future and who makes a positive difference.

Reflection: Thought leadership is a strategy.

_____

_____

_____

_____

_____

_____

_____

_____

_____

_____

_____

_____

_____

_____

_____

_____

Thought leadership requires, passion, commitment and courage,
as well as a willingness to think outside of the box.

_____ / _____ / _____
Month   Day   Year

153

NEXT STEPS:
BE A THOUGHT LEADER

MONDAY:

In reality, the term 'thought leader' has many definitions. Therefore, it is important to know what a thought leader is, and what it is not. Some people take a very expansive view of the term, wrapping internal strategy and corporate culture into the definition. Others have a more restricted definition.

Reflection: The thought leader is committed to learning more. There is value in being willing to learn and analyze new information and communicate it to others.

_____

_____

_____

_____

_____

_____

_____

_____

_____

_____

_____

_____

_____

_____

Control is not leadership. Management is not leadership.
Leadership is leadership.

NEXT STEPS:
BE A THOUGHT LEADER

A thought leader is the individual or firm that is viewed as the go-to individual or organization. They are recognized and accepted as being one of the foremost authorities in their specialty. They are a standout, as determined by others who have selected to classify them in that manner and utilize their services.

Reflection: As a thought leader, you cannot pretend to be an expert, you must be one.

_____

_____

_____

_____

_____

_____

_____

_____

_____

_____

_____

_____

_____

_____

_____

_____

Gain the respect of your colleagues, nation and world, by sharing quality ideas and focusing upon innovation, not sameness.

_____/_____/_____
Month   Day   Year

NEXT STEPS:
BE A THOUGHT LEADER

WEDNESDAY:

With this established recognition, a thought leader is an individual or firm who greatly benefits from this classification. People are in businesses to make money. Through the products and services of any business, they want to be excellent in their client deliverables and to be paid accordingly. Thought leadership is not devoid of making money.

Action Item: What two ideas would you place into the marketplace of ideas that you would find enriching for the good of the society?

_____

_____

_____

_____

_____

_____

_____

_____

_____

_____

_____

_____

_____

_____

Thought leadership requires that individual or organization think differently.

_____/_____/_____
Month   Day   Year

NEXT STEPS:
Be a Thought Leader

Thought leadership demonstrates that those with a certain skill set, with outstanding leadership, vision, Reflection and evaluation can move them forward. These attributes are valued by others as they gain empowerment in their initiative.

Reflection: Being a thought leader requires extra and hard work.

A thought leader moves us forward with expertise,
a track record, and clarity.

Month   Day   Year

NEXT STEPS:
BE A THOUGHT LEADER

FRIDAY:

Organizations have an on-going need for the offerings of a thought leader. Therefore, their work, although profitable, can be time-consuming. Being a thought leader requires that you are, in fact, authentic, dedicated to the task, and remain true to yourself. This is not an endeavor in which you can 'fake it, until you make it!'

Reflection: Being a thought leader means that you are following your passion in pursuing a body of work on topics that interest and intrigue you.

_____

_____

_____

_____

_____

_____

_____

_____

_____

_____

_____

_____

Standing alone, leadership qualities will not get you ahead.
People look for individuals who enjoy the respect of others.

NEXT STEPS:
Be a Thought Leader

Saturday:

SATURDAY:

Go beyond competence in your job, be an expert in a specific subject matter. If your information is accurate and valuable to those who seek it, they will benefit, and, of course, you will, as well. Accept the fact that you do not have a monopoly on 'knowing.' As you share your thoughts and ideas, keep it simple, so that others can understand and implement your ideas.

Reflection: Build a database of those people who are thought leaders and who have information that you can leverage.

_____

_____

_____

_____

_____

_____

_____

_____

_____

_____

_____

_____

There is no need to apologize because you have fresh ideas that problem solve and represent strategic thinking.

_____/_____/_____
Month   Day   Year

June

Workplace

"I suppose I could have stayed home and baked cookies and had teas,
but what I decided to do was to fulfill my profession which I entered
before my husband was in public life."
—Hillary Rodham Clinton

DIVERSITY:
The Common Denominator

All that you express comes back to you. Think about what you want for yourself. The features of diversity include age, race and ethnicity, gender, education, physical appearance, physical ability, culture, problem-solving, critical thinking, team building, military background, communication ability, income, the type of music and books appreciated, languages spoken, leadership abilities, conflict resolution skills, listening ability and ability to work with others.

Reflection: We learned that people have a common denominator. They are all different.

_____

_____

_____

_____

_____

_____

_____

_____

_____

_____

_____

_____

_____

Refuse to pigeonhole people. Truth is championed by intelligence.

_____/_____/_____
Month Day Year

DIVERSITY:
The Common Denominator

MONDAY:

Treat all people with respect, not just your family and friends. Some people think only intellect counts: knowing how to solve problems, knowing how to identify a better solution and apply it. But intellect must be accompanied by courage, love, friendship, compassion, and empathy.

Reflection: The greatest happiness comes when we know that we are loved in spite of ourselves.

In the midst of diversity, we are all simultaneously moving into the future, at the same speed.

DIVERSITY:
The Common Denominator

People are only as different as we make them out to be. We choose which characteristics are most important to us. Discover who you really are. The necessary comparison is to look at yourself in the mirror. You against you. It is that person whom you know best; whom you can influence the most; and whom you can expose to other people for your own self-improvement.

Reflection: Look for the best in people, things and situations.

We could learn a lot from crayons. Some are sharp, some are pretty, some are dull, and all are different colors. But, they all fit nicely into the same box.

163

_____/_____/_____
Month   Day   Year

DIVERSITY:
THE COMMON DENOMINATOR

WEDNESDAY:

Treat everyone fairly, without allowing favoritism to get in the way. Favoritism is a problem. When people are subjected to it, they become distrustful of the system. John Wooden, revered UCLA basketball coach, advanced his thoughts on people, "being different—treating everyone the same is the surest way to show favoritism."

Reflection: "There is nothing noble about being superior to others. The true nobility is in being superior to your previous self." –Hindu Proverb

_____

_____

_____

_____

_____

_____

_____

_____

_____

_____

_____

_____

_____

_____

Know yourself by knowing others. Your true self is, much larger and includes other people, and other cultures. It is with that understanding that our work and world will be better.

DIVERSITY:
THE COMMON DENOMINATOR

Remember that there is a discernible difference in having favorites, and playing favorites. Encourage others to maximize their potential. Ignoring diversity issues causes tension, loss of productivity and the loss of good people to other organizations. It is a lose-lose situation.

Action Item: List two times when you played 'favorites.'

_____

_____

_____

_____

_____

_____

_____

_____

_____

_____

_____

_____

_____

_____

Understand our differences, and act upon our commonalities.

165

DIVERSITY:
The Common Denominator

FRIDAY:

Half the people in the world are above/below average. So, what does that tell you? There is strength in the differences between us. There needs to be an acceptance of who and how we are. As humans, we all have aspirations, hopes and desires. We seek the best in ourselves and should look for the same in others. Learning this lesson earlier, rather than later.

Reflection: The test of courage comes when we are in the minority. The test of tolerance comes when we are in the majority.

_____

_____

_____

_____

_____

_____

_____

_____

_____

_____

_____

_____

"Diversity…is not casual liberal tolerance…It is not polite accommodation…Diversity is…the sometimes painful awareness that other people…have as much integrity of being…as you do. …We are all meant to be here together."
– William M. Chase, "The Language of Action"

DIVERSITY:
THE COMMON DENOMINATOR

Be honest with others. It will help you to avoid conflict and controversy. Give quality time to thinking about your preferences and prejudices and make a decision as to whether you are limiting yourself by pre-judging other people. Differences should enrich, not disquiet.

Reflection: Ask others for help when you need it.

_____

_____

_____

_____

_____

_____

_____

_____

_____

_____

_____

_____

_____

Everyone in the world smiles in the same language.

_____/_____/_____
Month   Day   Year

WORKING FROM THE BOTTOM OF THE PILE

SUNDAY:

When your house, car, desk at home and work are a cluttered mess, there is a good chance that your relationships and self-esteem aren't far behind. Setting aside time during your day to clean up, organize, and de-clutter can make a world of difference. Paper does not need to be your enemy.

Reflection: Start everyday with your most important task, leaving other assignments undone. They, too, will become a priority.

_____

_____

_____

_____

_____

_____

_____

_____

_____

_____

_____

_____

_____

_____

Take a course in time management.
Work it into your schedule.

WORKING FROM THE BOTTOM OF THE PILE

If you feel totally overwhelmed by the amount of work calling your name, then focus on it one bit at a time. Prioritize. Stay on your established schedule. Catch-up is a very hard game to play. Look for ways of freeing yourself of unnecessary, stressful projects. Determine whether every single item on your to-do list will benefit you.

Reflection: Make certain that you don't like work so much that rather than doing it, you are simply watching it.

_____

_____

_____

_____

_____

_____

_____

_____

_____

_____

_____

_____

Focused action beats brilliance.

_____/_____/_____
Month Day Year

WORKING FROM THE BOTTOM OF THE PILE

TUESDAY:

Life isn't easy. We have to fall down many times before we finally learn to fly. Designate three boxes, 'keep,' 'toss' or 'place' the paper in a box entitled 'elsewhere.' These boxes do not include filing time and/or things that have to be taken to another room. First things first, place each item into the designated box.

Action Item: Take some quality time, to move, clean out and get rid of everything you don't need.

Do not confuse motion and progress.

WORKING FROM THE BOTTOM OF THE PILE

Also, remember that each project, contract, initiative, proposal or task that you are working on deserves its own labeled binder. There is great value in following this method. When you have to reference that subject, everything on the topic will be already pre-arranged in chronological order, in your binder

Reflection: Find and eliminate wasteful actions in your life.

_____

_____

_____

_____

_____

_____

_____

_____

_____

_____

_____

_____

_____

_____

_____

"Live each day as if it be your last."
– Marcus Aurelius, 140 AD

_____/_____/_____
Month   Day   Year

WORKING FROM THE BOTTOM OF THE PILE

THURSDAY:

Why are you procrastinating? Rather than take on the task, are you ignoring reality? The task will be right there staring at you, until you make a decision to tackle it. Don't act as if there is a dreaded disease in your inbox, and you want to avoid it like the plague.

Reflection: If you can do it in five minutes, do it right then. Don't delay. Otherwise, you are planting the seed for your inbox to grow.

_____

_____

_____

_____

_____

_____

_____

_____

_____

_____

_____

_____

_____

Living your life without a plan is like watching television with
someone else holding the remote control.

WORKING FROM THE BOTTOM OF THE PILE

Friday:

FRIDAY:

Worry creeps in and it won't let go. Start now. Unless you face it, you are allowing your molehill to turn into a mountain. Isolate your strengths and weaknesses. Identify the most difficult part of the work, versus the part that is easier; and the time of day that works best for you to apply yourself to the task.

Reflection: Sit down and organize your thought process.

_____

_____

_____

_____

_____

_____

_____

_____

_____

_____

_____

_____

_____

_____

Seek to master your time. Most people overestimate what they can accomplish in a month — and underestimate what they can achieve in a year. Get started.

_____/_____/_____
Month   Day   Year

WORKING FROM THE BOTTOM OF THE PILE

SATURDAY:

Don't allow difficult tasks to frustrate you or to become your Achilles heel. Take the time and give the attention to doing something every day. Ultimately, you will clean and clear your inbox. You will benefit by collecting things in as few places as possible. Clean up and clear out on a regular basis.

Action Item: List two reasons why you have previously chosen procrastination over action.

_____

_____

_____

_____

_____

_____

_____

_____

_____

_____

_____

_____

Know the true value of time. Snatch, seize, and enjoy
every moment of your time. Refuse to engage in idleness,
laziness or procrastination.

LAGNIAPPE (LAN-YAP) (A little bit more)

Every day we are exposed to businesses that make us wonder whether the customer counts at all. Significantly, as the customer, we know that but for the customer, the employee would not have a job. The only person who seems uninformed of that fact is the employee.

Action Item: Name the situation in which you felt most devalued, disrespected or denied as a customer.

_____

_____

_____

_____

_____

_____

_____

_____

_____

_____

_____

_____

_____

Adopt the standard of excellence without excuse.

175

_____/_____/_____
Month   Day   Year

LAGNIAPPE (LAN-YAP) (A little bit more)

MONDAY:

Whether at the grocery store, post office, physician's office, DMV, or placing a takeout order, and you arrive to pick it up, there is no record that the order was ever placed. Something is missing in customer care. Employees do not listen to the customer. Many are engaged in their own conversation with a friend and that is much more important than transacting your business. They are untrained and disinterested.

Reflection: When a person excels in his job, how do you demonstrate your appreciation?

_____

_____

_____

_____

_____

_____

_____

_____

_____

_____

_____

_____

_____

Make the impossible inevitable.

LAGNIAPPE (LAN-YAP) (A little bit more)

An employee's poor attitude and/or bad behavior may result in them offering an apology; they may say, "I'm sorry," and that is exactly what they are, "sorry!"

Reflection: How do you respond when you encounter a poor attitude or bad behavior?

_____

_____

_____

_____

_____

_____

_____

_____

_____

_____

_____

_____

_____

Customers have a choice.
Rarely is one business the only business in town.

_____/_____/_____
Month Day Year

LAGNIAPPE (LAN-YAP) (A little bit more)

WEDNESDAY:

Customers may come through the door, but the larger issue is whether they will be a repeat customer to increase the bottom line. Focus on all of those businesses, large and small, that have a very weak customer service record, because their customers would rather not be bothered with the effort of trying to use their product or service.

Action Item: List three attributes of an employee that simply, "makes your day!"

_____

_____

_____

_____

_____

_____

_____

_____

_____

_____

_____

_____

_____

_____

Treat all criticism as if it is constructive.
It will help you to grow.

_____/_____/_____
Month   Day   Year

LAGNIAPPE (LAN-YAP) (A little bit more)

There is great merit in learning the advantage in under-promising and over-delivering. Businesses, in the public or private sector should use this mantra as a policy. The customer should be able to expect reliability and accountability. Now, the customer should expect a little bit more, (lagniappe) which includes a trained and informed staff.

Reflection: In your view, what is meant by the statement, "The customer is always right?"

_____

_____

_____

_____

_____

_____

_____

_____

_____

_____

_____

_____

To accomplish great things, think big, dream,
plan, act, and believe.

____/____/____
Month Day Year

179

LAGNIAPPE (LAN-YAP) (A little bit more)

In Louisiana, by definition, a lagniappe is a small gift given to a customer by a merchant at the time of a purchase or something given or obtained gratuitously as a winning gesture. It is the seller's way of throwing in a little extra. Whether on the Gulf Coast of the United States, North Africa, rural France, or Holland the term and practice is familiar. It is the equivalent of the thirteenth donut that makes up 'the baker's dozen.'

Action Item: List two examples when an employee or business has actually engaged in 'lagniappe' for you or your purchase.

_____

_____

_____

_____

_____

_____

_____

_____

_____

_____

_____

_____

_____

_____

In life, giving from your heart is the thing
that makes the difference.

_____/_____/_____
Month   Day   Year

LAGNIAPPE (LAN-YAP) (A little bit more)

Simply put, we need the workforce to give...just a little bit more, employers and employees, need to take the next step. Be kind, courteous, efficient, effective, appreciative, and informed. Lagniappe. Give a little bit more. A customer is waiting.

Reflection: What role do you have as a customer during the identifiable decline in quality customer service?

_____

_____

_____

_____

_____

_____

_____

_____

_____

_____

_____

_____

_____

_____

Being angry is not worth it, when being helpful is an option.

_____/_____/_____
Month   Day   Year

THE ENEMY:
Procrastination

SUNDAY:

Every day we find ourselves wondering where the time has gone. There is always so much to do, in so little time. We arrive earlier and earlier to work, and yet, the inbox is still piled high, and all those requests of 'can you, will you' have gone unanswered and/or work goes unfinished.

Action Item: If you could add more hours to the day, provide your formula for work balance. How many hours are required for your formula?

_____

_____

_____

_____

_____

_____

_____

_____

_____

_____

_____

_____

Value your time. To do so, shows that you value yourself.

THE ENEMY:
PROCRASTINATION

Typically, it seems that we have a great tendency to put off what needs to be done now. We make a decision that we can goof off in school, and still make the grade; perform in an average manner on the job, and still get the promotion; or leave a little late, and still beat the traffic.

Action Item: List two procrastination tendencies that you have that have served to your detriment.

_____

_____

_____

_____

_____

_____

_____

_____

_____

_____

_____

_____

_____

_____

If you lose days of work by what you fail to do,
those days are gone forever.

_____/_____/_____
Month   Day   Year

THE ENEMY:
PROCRASTINATION

TUESDAY:

Procrastination can become a pattern and practice. You can delay with such expertise you may think that it is an art. You actually wrote the manual on getting in just under the sound of the buzzer.

Reflection: Share your 'best counsel' with those who have not yet realized or accepted that time is of the essence!

_____

_____

_____

_____

_____

_____

_____

_____

_____

_____

_____

_____

_____

_____

If you want to get something done: Begin.

THE ENEMY:
PROCRASTINATION

There are significant disadvantages in living on the cutting edge. Your attitude and strategic plan is focused upon being exactly on time, not early; to make an acceptable grade, not to set the standard; and to be good enough, not to excel.

Reflection: If you made a decision to be focused as the one whose example is worthy for others to follow, what are the advantages to you?

_____

_____

_____

_____

_____

_____

_____

_____

_____

_____

_____

_____

_____

Procrastination will show you that:
1. You need to do your work today.
2. Tomorrow will be your today, tomorrow

_____/_____/_____
Month   Day   Year

THE ENEMY:
PROCRASTINATION

THURSDAY:

Notwithstanding how well intentioned you are, all of us procrastinate. It's the ugly truth. We avoid tackling the tough reports, laborious forms that must be filled out or completing a difficult assignment. Every day is a part of the countdown as we avoid, de-prioritize and simply refuse to get the job done. It is easier and wiser to just do it. Later can be now.

Reflection: Are you held hostage by the phrase that, "misery loves company?" Are you willing to break away from the pack?

_____

_____

_____

_____

_____

_____

_____

_____

_____

_____

_____

_____

_____

Someday is not a day of the week.

_____

THE ENEMY:
PROCRASTINATION

What can you do to become more efficient with so many 'essential' things to do? First, admit that you procrastinate. Decide what benefits will accrue to you when you complete a task in a timely manner. Work on a specific schedule for getting things done. Be accountable to yourself and to those to whom you have made a commitment.

Reflection: Make a statement as to the importance of standing by your words, actions and follow through.

_____

_____

_____

_____

_____

_____

_____

_____

_____

_____

_____

_____

_____

Money comes and money goes, but time is irreplaceable.

_____/_____/_____
Month   Day   Year

THE ENEMY:
PROCRASTINATION

SATURDAY:

When you complete any task, give yourself a pat on the back. Pause and reflect as to the method you used to achieve the task. Remember. You are on the clock.

Reflection: When you set the clock for every 30 minutes for an hour and a half, is that, procrastination? Why?

_____

_____

_____

_____

_____

_____

_____

_____

_____

_____

_____

_____

An uncompleted task will really tire you out.

July

Work Place II

"I think women have proved themselves beyond a shadow of a doubt that they are as capable and as confident in delivering results. The "B" word…babies or biology is a complicated one. Because it doesn't mean that women can't do the work, it means that women have a point, a period in their life of maybe…depending on how many children they have, of 5 to 10 years where they have a lessened amount of availability."

– Suzy Welch

THE RUMOR MILL

Sunday:

SUNDAY:

It simply is not true. But, who knew? There's an element of gossip present in every social enterprise. Gossip is 'making a derogatory statement about someone to a third person where the opinion of that person is diminished in the eyes of the third person.' Light gossip and a few comments here and there probably won't hurt anyone; a pervasive culture of rumormongering and trash talking is detrimental to everyone.

Action Item: Identify two times when your behavior of engaging in gossip hurt another person.

_____

_____

_____

_____

_____

_____

_____

_____

_____

_____

_____

_____

_____

_____

_____

Don't worry about trying to explain your thoughts,
ideas or actions. People make their own conclusions.

THE RUMOR MILL

Gossip destroys morale, creates negative energy at work and stops coworkers from becoming a united team. In the world of organizational politics, gossip is prevalent, particularly in times of uncertainty. People are anxious, ambivalent and insecure. Gossip poisons the workplace and causes negativity, bitterness and discontent.

Reflection: When you were the subject of gossip, how did you respond?

_____

_____

_____

_____

_____

_____

_____

_____

_____

_____

_____

_____

_____

_____

_____

Everybody has an opinion notwithstanding what you say or do.

_____

_____/_____/_____
Month   Day   Year

191

THE RUMOR MILL

TUESDAY:

The idea is not to say anything hurtful behind someone's back. Cut the drama. Corporate culture does not need or welcome preventable office politics and gossip.

Reflection: What is the importance of you being helpful, not hurtful to others?

_____

_____

_____

_____

_____

_____

_____

_____

_____

_____

_____

_____

_____

Where do you find the truth in gossip?

THE RUMOR MILL

Wednesday:

Treat everyone fairly, without allowing favoritism to get in the way. Raise your thoughts, ideas and concerns, without simultaneously feeling that you are backstabbing or wallowing in a gossipy snake pit. Open communication channels are desired and deserved. Stop the rumor mill. Enough already!

Action Item: How can you best curtail a rumor mill?

_____

_____

_____

_____

_____

_____

_____

_____

_____

_____

_____

_____

_____

It may be unreasonable, even unexpected,
but time may heal all wounds.

193

___/___/___
Month Day Year

THE RUMOR MILL

THURSDAY:

Make certain that you are not leaning on the water cooler with the next in-office updates. For example, if you are willing to discuss a missed deadline, a team that did not complete the project, or a relationship that you thought was solidly moving forward that fell apart at the seams, messes created by on-going dialogue 'he said, she said' that creates the lightening flash rumor, you may be the next topic of discussion. What goes around really does come around.

Reflection: Gossip is a demonstration of someone else's inabilities.

_____

_____

_____

_____

_____

_____

_____

_____

_____

_____

_____

_____

_____

_____

_____

There is a lot of truth that should not be shared with others.

THE RUMOR MILL

Analyze why human beings can be so mean-spirited toward others. It is that very conduct and behavior that is disruptive, disheartening and discourteous. In other words, lies make their own way and arrive at their destination much faster than the truth.

Reflection: Are you courageous enough to tell the truth and stand by your position?

_____

_____

_____

_____

_____

_____

_____

_____

_____

_____

_____

_____

_____

If you can't say something nice about somebody, be quiet.

_____/_____/_____
Month   Day   Year

THE RUMOR MILL

SATURDAY:

Words that cause wounds may be more prevalent than anything that bleeds. However, know that you do not have a monopoly on being the target of those who would seek to attack your best self. It is their weakness and lack of character that is held up to the light. Let that, my friend, be your satisfaction and encouragement.

Action Item: What two indicators did you have that a colleague or a so-called friend was learning and sharing your business to your detriment?

_____

_____

_____

_____

_____

_____

_____

_____

_____

_____

_____

_____

_____

_____

Those who gossip with you will ultimately gossip about you.

LEAD, FOLLOW OR GET OUT OF THE WAY

Those who are willing to sign up as the leader can prepare to also have slings and arrows hurled against them. It comes with the territory. Early on, you must keep reminding yourself of the greater good, the higher calling, and the benefit that will come from your leadership. Leadership without action is apathy.

Reflection: Identify whether you believe that you are a leader or a follower. Why?

_____

_____

_____

_____

_____

_____

_____

_____

_____

_____

_____

_____

_____

_____

_____

Leaders know that you cannot make a brand new start,
but you can make a brand new ending,

_____

197

LEAD, FOLLOW OR GET OUT OF THE WAY

MONDAY:

During the most difficult times, many call for better, wiser, and more available leadership. Leaders are able to identify their own strengths and surround themselves with people who can get the job done. The goal is to create more leaders, not followers.

Action Item: List four reasons why there is a lack of quality leadership.

_____

_____

_____

_____

_____

_____

_____

_____

_____

_____

_____

_____

_____

_____

_____

_____

_____

Working with others is a skill. Master it.

_____

LEAD, FOLLOW OR GET OUT OF THE WAY

TUESDAY:

Good leaders are inspiring and have a sense of certainty. A leader is often required to be a change agent, to shift the paradigm and to break the routine, as the individuals whom they are leading, are eager to listen to their decision making. Once a decision is made, that leader must be prepared to accept the fact that acts have consequences.

Action Item: Describe how you have sought to inspire those whom you have lead and the result.

_____

_____

_____

_____

_____

_____

_____

_____

_____

_____

_____

_____

_____

_____

Think about anyone great that you know. You have exactly the same number of hours that they were given. Act.

____/____/____
Month   Day   Year

199

LEAD, FOLLOW OR GET OUT OF THE WAY

WEDNESDAY:

Leadership is neither charisma nor power. Many have personality, and they are likable, but they are not leaders. Power may even be the opposite of leadership. Leaders make assessments of those around them, and empower them to use their talents, skills and abilities.

Action Item: Give your profile of leadership.

_____

_____

_____

_____

_____

_____

_____

_____

_____

_____

_____

_____

_____

LEAD. Think as a visionary who meets others act their point of need, without judgment.

LEAD, FOLLOW OR GET OUT OF THE WAY

Leadership is not micro-management. Leaders listen attentively, and they actually value what their team members are saying. They understand that it is not all about them. Leaders are engaged in honesty and fair dealing. Thus, they are trustworthy and believable.

Action Item: Describe a situation when you stepped outside of your personal/professional interest for those whom you were leading.

_____

_____

_____

_____

_____

_____

_____

_____

_____

_____

_____

_____

_____

_____

_____

In leadership, give yourself a break and stay on target.

_____/_____/_____
Month   Day   Year

LEAD, FOLLOW OR GET OUT OF THE WAY

FRIDAY:

A leader has the vision and courage to travel the unchartered course, and to take the responsibility that others may avoid. Leadership is not always pleasant or easy, but a leader faces the music, even when they do not like the tune. Set an example of sharing in the blame for those things that did not go exactly as planned, and take a little less than your share of the credit for a job well done.

Action Item: List two situations when you, as the leader, had to accept the fact that the 'buck stops with you.'

_____

_____

_____

_____

_____

_____

_____

_____

_____

_____

_____

_____

_____

Leadership requires that you leave your comfort zone.

LEAD, FOLLOW OR GET OUT OF THE WAY

SATURDAY:

Real leadership is about real change. Learn to treat people beyond their own expectations and acceptance of who they think they are. Treat them at the level of their potential. By doing so, you empower them to get out of their own way.

Action Item: When did you discover that 'empowerment' is more than a buzz phrase? List two lessons learned.

_____

_____

_____

_____

_____

_____

_____

_____

_____

_____

_____

_____

_____

_____

_____

In leadership, make certain that you understand your options.

_____

_____/_____/_____
Month   Day   Year

READING BETWEEN THE LINES

Sunday:

SUNDAY:

In life, we have many circumstances to evaluate. We have the responsibility not to take everything literally. We have to be or become a critical thinker of all relevant factors. Seek to understand someone's real feelings or intentions from what they say, write or do.

Reflection: Imagine a document that is single-spaced. Then, the lines are adjusted and the actual message is revealed. Regarding your life, what is the message?

_____

_____

_____

_____

_____

_____

_____

_____

_____

_____

_____

_____

Critical thinking is essential. Be certain that you don't take everything at face value.

_____/_____/_____
Month   Day   Year

204

READING BETWEEN THE LINES

It is essential to be honest and to adhere to a standard of integrity. Find the deeper meaning. Listen and learn from what is said, and what isn't. Tap your intuitive understanding and go beyond what is said and what is really meant.

Action Item: Identify two times when you have said what you meant and meant what you said.

_____

_____

_____

_____

_____

_____

_____

_____

_____

_____

_____

_____

Think about what wasn't said. At times,
it is the hidden message that is most important.

_____/_____/_____
Month   Day   Year

READING BETWEEN THE LINES

Tuesday:

TUESDAY:

Practice makes permanent. Here are some examples just in case you didn't already know: "I don't care what anyone thinks." –MEANING– "I really do care what people think, maybe too much." "It's not you, it's me." –MEANING– "Let's not kid ourselves; you're definitely the reason we're breaking up."

Reflection: Identify the value add of selecting your words to represent your true feelings. Is there also any disadvantage in doing so?

_____

_____

_____

_____

_____

_____

_____

_____

_____

_____

_____

_____

_____

_____

_____

Actions speak louder than words.

_____

READING BETWEEN THE LINES

"What is your career?"—MEANING—"Do you have a job and what is it so that I can determine whether you are on the way up and in my social-economic class." "Exams that require writing are too difficult"—MEANING—"I am disinclined to apply the time to excel." "It has been my pleasure to meet you." —MEANING—"I am looking for someone else in the room, so that I can determine if they are more important than you."

Reflection: Have you ever underestimated the person who was standing right in front of you, and opted instead to spend your time with others whom you mistakenly thought to be more influential?

_____

_____

_____

_____

_____

_____

_____

_____

_____

_____

_____

_____

Subliminal messages can make you curious, even suspicious.
Don't get angry, it is not worth your energy.

_____/_____/_____
Month   Day   Year

READING BETWEEN THE LINES

THURSDAY:

People are strong. Some are inconsistent in their behavior, so you don't really know when and whether they will be hot or cold, in a good mood or bad mood, helpful or hurtful. Therefore, believe in yourself. At times, you will be your best or only ally.

Reflection: Why is it important for you to have self-confidence and to be your own friend?

_____

_____

_____

_____

_____

_____

_____

_____

_____

_____

_____

_____

_____

The real question is not who is going to let you,
but who is going to stop you.

READING BETWEEN THE LINES

Stay in touch with yourself. It is very easy to feel the disappointment of others or to discredit them. Go through life with clean hands. When you point a finger, at least three others are pointing back at you.

Reflection: What is the importance of other people in your life? Why or why not?

_____

_____

_____

_____

_____

_____

_____

_____

_____

_____

_____

_____

_____

_____

Don't take the shortcut. Finish what you started.

_____/_____/_____
Month   Day   Year

READING BETWEEN THE LINES

SATURDAY:

Take comfort in knowing that some people are genuine. They are supportive, attractive and authentic. The good news is that it has nothing to do with their image; it is how they are inside.

Reflection: Identify the person who you think has the most outstanding qualities—inside. Why?

_____

_____

_____

_____

_____

_____

_____

_____

_____

_____

_____

_____

Always strive to step out of your comfort zone.

WORKPLACE JOKES

All questions, comments, concerns, complaints, frustrations, irritations, aggravations, insinuations, allegations, accusations, contemplations, consternations or input should be directed elsewhere. Perhaps for years you have been blaming yourself for being tired from a lack of sleep, and too much pressure from your job, but now you know the real reason: You are tired because you are overworked.

Reflection: What do you do to renew when you feel that you are overworked?

_____

_____

_____

_____

_____

_____

_____

_____

_____

_____

_____

A job is more than an income—it's an important part of who you are. A career transition of any sort is an unsettling experience.

_____/_____/_____
Month   Day   Year

WORKPLACE JOKES

MONDAY:

The population of this country is 237 million. 104 million are retired. That leaves 133 million to do the work. There are 85 million in school, which leaves 48 million to do the work.

Reflection: When you are self-employed, every day when you wake up you are unemployed, so don't put the alarm clock on snooze.

_____

_____

_____

_____

_____

_____

_____

_____

_____

_____

_____

_____

_____

_____

Find a job that you like, and you add five days to every week.

WORKPLACE JOKES

There are 29 million employed by the federal government, leaving 19 million to do the work. 2.8 million are in the Armed Forces, which leaves 16.2 million to do the work.

Reflection: "The difference between a job and a career is the difference between forty and sixty hours a week." —Robert Frost

_____

_____

_____

_____

_____

_____

_____

_____

_____

_____

_____

_____

_____

Accomplishing the impossible means only that the boss will add it to your regular duties.

_____/_____/_____
Month Day   Year

WORKPLACE JOKES

WEDNESDAY:

Take from the total the 14,800,000 people who work for State and City Governments and that leaves 1.4 million to do the work.

Reflection: Law of the Alibi: If you tell the boss you were late for work because you had a flat tire, the very next morning you will have a flat tire.

_____

_____

_____

_____

_____

_____

_____

_____

_____

_____

_____

_____

_____

Wednesdays are like Mondays in the middle of the week.

WORKPLACE JOKES

THURSDAY:

At any given time, there are 188,000 people in hospitals, leaving 1,212,000 to do the work.

Reflection: Today many people have a B.A., an M.A. or a PhD, but they don't have a J.O.B.!

_____
_____
_____
_____
_____
_____
_____
_____
_____
_____
_____
_____
_____
_____

*Executive ability is deciding quickly and
getting somebody else to do the work.*

215

___/___/___
Month   Day   Year

WORKPLACE JOKES

FRIDAY:

Now, there are 1,211,998 people in prisons.

Reflection: The closest to perfection a person ever comes is when they fill out a job application form.

_____

_____

_____

_____

_____

_____

_____

_____

_____

_____

_____

_____

_____

_____

Excellence is an attitude.

_____

WORKPLACE JOKES

That leaves just two people to do the work. You and me. And you're sitting at your computer reading jokes.

Reflection: Being intentional advances your career. How?

_____

_____

_____

_____

_____

_____

_____

_____

_____

_____

_____

In life, you may not get everything you work for, but you will work for everything that you get.

217

August

Leadership

"Start by starting."
—Meryl Streep

COURAGEOUS LEADERSHIP

Courage means different things in different situations. It may be to make a decision and act, even when you're operating in unfamiliar territory. Courage may be to weigh the pros and cons and, even when there is no clear cut solution, you still make a decision and take the appropriate action. Face whatever you are going through. Every person can lead.

Reflection Item: Identify the greatest example of your personal leadership.

_____

_____

_____

_____

_____

_____

_____

_____

_____

_____

_____

_____

Take the time to be what you ought to be.

_____/_____/_____
Month   Day   Year

COURAGEOUS LEADERSHIP

MONDAY:

We often hear about visionary leadership. A visionary leader will lead teams, organizations or followers where they need to be. The leader is believable because they set an example by what they are willing to do.

Reflection: Are you a visionary leader? If so, how? If not, why not?

_____

_____

_____

_____

_____

_____

_____

_____

_____

_____

_____

_____

_____

Small steps in leadership,
can give major benefits in lessons learned.

_____/_____/_____
Month Day Year

220

COURAGEOUS LEADERSHIP

As a leader, you must know your own beliefs. The requirement of courage is often not convenient. It may be fleeting as you take on the battle to climb upwards to face one battle after another. Take on the burden of leadership. The banner is to learn as you go. As a result, you will be more confident, stronger and wiser. Persevere.

Action Item: What are the greatest three assets of leadership?

_____

_____

_____

_____

_____

_____

_____

_____

_____

_____

_____

_____

_____

_____

Leadership is something within that no one can effect from without.

_____/_____/_____
Month   Day   Year

COURAGEOUS LEADERSHIP

WEDNESDAY:

To lead rarely means that you will be in a safe harbor. Leadership most often will involve taking a risk, rocking the boat, making tough decisions, and being very strategic when others would chose to be haphazard. An organization avoids leaders who are anxious, ambivalent or unsure. People welcome leadership that is calm, deliberate and dependable.

Reflection: Leadership means that you will rarely be able to stay near the shoreline.

_____

_____

_____

_____

_____

_____

_____

_____

_____

_____

_____

_____

_____

_____

_____

Discover what calms you. Visualize it. Lead.

COURAGEOUS LEADERSHIP

It takes courage to release the familiar, and to embrace the new. There is more security in that which is known and expected. In movement, there is life, and in change there is power.

Reflection: In leadership, expect the unexpected.

_____

_____

_____

_____

_____

_____

_____

_____

_____

_____

_____

_____

When you make a mistake, admit it.
Then, correct it and refuse to stand on your pride.

_____/_____/_____
Month   Day   Year

COURAGEOUS LEADERSHIP

FRIDAY:

"In Germany, they came first for the Communists, and I didn't speak up because I wasn't a Communist. Then they came for the Jews, and I didn't speak up because I wasn't a Jew. Then they came for the trade unionists, and I didn't speak up because I wasn't a trade unionist. Then they came for the Catholics, and I didn't speak up, because I was a Protestant. Then they came for me, and by that time no one was left to speak up."
–Martin Niemöller, German Lutheran Pastor.

Action Item: Identify two situations when you waited too long to become involved for the others as well as yourself.

_____

_____

_____

_____

_____

_____

_____

_____

_____

_____

_____

_____

_____

The world is full of frustrations and disappointments,
but the challenge is to overcome them.

COURAGEOUS LEADERSHIP

Leadership requires great risk. We need people in our lives with whom we can be as open as possible. To have real conversation with people involves courage and risk. The reward for genuine communication will be the empowerment of others who will, enrich organizations, communities, and individuals.

Reflection: Establish and maintain quality lines of communication.

_____

_____

_____

_____

_____

_____

_____

_____

_____

_____

_____

_____

_____

_____

Pause. Make an assessment of your problems and then make a decision as to just how serious your problems are.

225

_____/_____/_____
Month Day Year

MENTORING:
SEND THE ELEVATOR BACK DOWN

SUNDAY:

Women are significantly behind men when it comes to how they effectively use networks to get ahead in their careers. It is sad, but true, that many women who are in position to be a catalytic force to help other women, are held hostage by their own need to be a 'queen bee.' She wants to be viewed as 'the only one at the top,' and she does little or nothing to empower others.

Action Item: List examples of those individuals you have assisted in their careers. How did you help them?

_____

_____

_____

_____

_____

_____

_____

_____

_____

_____

_____

_____

_____

_____

_____

_____

_____

Remember: Once you reach the top, send the elevator back down.

_____

____/____/_____
Month Day Year

226

MENTORING:
SEND THE ELEVATOR BACK DOWN

It is a mistake to think that, in school or the workplace, you made it on your own. It is a mistake to conclude that others must find the path to success for themselves. The truth is, however, that the phrase is correct, "No man is an island and No woman is either." Everybody needs somebody.

Reflection: What person in your life moved you beyond your own expectations? How?

_____

_____

_____

_____

_____

_____

_____

_____

_____

_____

_____

_____

_____

_____

*"Do all the good you can...By all the means you can...In all the
ways you can...In all the places you can...To all the people you
can...As long as you can."*
–John Wesley

227

MENTORING:
SEND THE ELEVATOR BACK DOWN

TUESDAY:

To help other female leaders maximize their potential is a relay. It is neither a marathon nor a sprint. The required exposure and experience is on-going. It is a strategic process, not a program.

Reflection: How do women hurt themselves by hurting each other?

_____

_____

_____

_____

_____

_____

_____

_____

_____

_____

_____

_____

_____

_____

_____

_____

Many have gone much further than they ever thought they could, because someone else thought they could.

MENTORING:
SEND THE ELEVATOR BACK DOWN

Establishing a mentor-protégée relationship can be a slippery slope. Women and minorities are often not at the senior management level, and some of those who are may not be inclined to take on one more task as they assist in preparing you for the line of succession.

Action Item: Identify the rewards of mentoring others and assisting them in becoming the individual who has the courage to be their best.

_____

_____

_____

_____

_____

_____

_____

_____

_____

_____

_____

_____

Try it. It works. Be on the giving end.

229

_____/_____/_____
Month   Day   Year

MENTORING:
SEND THE ELEVATOR BACK DOWN

THURSDAY:

Learn the informal pathways, networks, games, and activities of those who seem to propel to the top. Those things may include, and not be limited to, specific career training, conference attendance, affinity groups or playing golf. In sum, all business conversations and decisions are not made in the office. You have to go where the action is.

Action Item: Name three informal strategies to reach career goals.

_____

_____

_____

_____

_____

_____

_____

_____

_____

_____

_____

_____

_____

_____

_____

_____

_____

If you really want to feel good, help somebody else.

MENTORING:
SEND THE ELEVATOR BACK DOWN

The 'glass ceiling' is more than an abstract concept. It is real. To break this barrier, it is expected that you will have the fortitude, willpower and courage to go to the next levels.

Action Item: Specifically, identify your workplace 'glass ceilings' and how you crashed them.

_____

_____

_____

_____

_____

_____

_____

_____

_____

_____

_____

_____

Women don't have flashes, they have power surges.

_____/_____/_____
Month   Day   Year

MENTORING:
SEND THE ELEVATOR BACK DOWN

SATURDAY:

In the workplace, if you have a real interest in moving forward, you must be able to assess the culture and politics in the organization. Equally important, you will need to leverage a support network of other women that will increase your own understanding of what works and what doesn't.

Reflection: How have you learned organizational culture? How did learning the culture, benefit your career?

_____

_____

_____

_____

_____

_____

_____

_____

_____

_____

_____

_____

_____

Organizational politics means that you must know, and know that you know.

NOT ON MY WATCH

The level of disrespect and challenge people heap upon others has given rise to strong statements of what and when people will tolerate or accept. In fact, many take offense, and will adamantly share that they will not accept objectionable attitudes, commentary or behavior. They state, "Not on my watch."

Reflection: As a servant leader, do you find your conversational tone or leadership style to be 'in your face?'

_____

_____

_____

_____

_____

_____

_____

_____

_____

_____

_____

_____

_____

Be an optimist. Half the people in the world are above average.

_____/_____/_____
Month   Day   Year

NOT ON MY WATCH

MONDAY:

There is an expectation that when someone else is acting up or acting out, when they are embarrassing themselves, it can be expected that the red light comes with the declaration, that if the proposed actions were to take place, it may happen at any other time, but it won't occur during your leadership. You will move forward with dedication, determination and proven judgment.

Reflection: Do you think that your capability statement exceeds others?

_____

_____

_____

_____

_____

_____

_____

_____

_____

_____

_____

_____

_____

_____

Always look for ways to improve yourself.

_____

_____/_____/_____
Month Day Year

234

NOT ON MY WATCH

This expression of 'not on my watch' is used to mean that you are not cowed or intimidated by anyone. You are in a position to stand up for yourself, strike back and/or take revenge when someone is challenging you or someone else.

Reflection: Do you feel that you must be the one to give direction to others?

_____

_____

_____

_____

_____

_____

_____

_____

_____

_____

_____

_____

_____

_____

Always remember that you are unique, just like everybody else.

_____/_____/_____
Month   Day   Year

NOT ON MY WATCH

WEDNESDAY:

It is hard work to say the right thing, at the right time to the right people, with the right words. Your passion may not be theirs, therefore, you must seek balance in what you expect them to do and how.

Reflection: Do you have room in your personality for the thoughts, ideas and actions of others?

_____

_____

_____

_____

_____

_____

_____

_____

_____

_____

_____

_____

_____

_____

_____

First, we make our habits, and then our habits make us.

_____

_____/_____/_____
Month   Day   Year

236

NOT ON MY WATCH

Your assessment of what you will accept can be very revealing as to how you work with individuals. Don't dictate. Be certain that others take ownership of a philosophy or ideology that helps everyone, not just that which responds to your preference or prejudice.

Action Item: List two examples of how you have adjusted your personality to be inclusive of others.

_____

_____

_____

_____

_____

_____

_____

_____

_____

_____

_____

_____

_____

_____

Resist the temptation to micro-manage people.

_____/_____/_____
Month   Day   Year

NOT ON MY WATCH

FRIDAY:

You cannot control what happens to you, but you can control your attitude toward what happens to you. Master change, rather than to allow it to master you.

Reflection: Do you believe your life demonstrates a noteworthy legacy?

_____

_____

_____

_____

_____

_____

_____

_____

_____

_____

_____

_____

_____

_____

Master the situation. Use words that demonstrate your consciousness and control.

NOT ON MY WATCH

Be very certain that the values, beliefs and behaviors that you demonstrate, helps others. Weigh whether there is merit in your insistence upon having the last word.

Reflection: Diversity is an advantage. How often do you demonstrate your respect and appreciation for others?

_____

_____

_____

_____

_____

_____

_____

_____

_____

_____

_____

_____

_____

Apply reason. It is the sign of an intelligent person.

_____/_____/_____
Month   Day   Year

THE SOLUTION:
OVER, AROUND, UNDER OR THROUGH

SUNDAY:

Don't take your eye off the goal. You are not alone. Every human being faces opportunities and obstacles, whether in the personal or professional arena.

For example, be encouraged, if you have ever failed, you are in good company. Persons who persist when it seems as if there is no way up and out, typically discover that their fortitude, and stick-to-it-tiveness will help find the answer.

Reflection: Success is often found by using several alternative methods of problem-solving.

_____

_____

_____

_____

_____

_____

_____

_____

_____

_____

_____

_____

"You've got to continue to grow,
or you're just like last night's cornbread—stale and dry."
- Loretta Lynn

THE SOLUTION:
OVER, AROUND, UNDER OR THROUGH

Obstacles are like mountains; they're not going to move themselves. You have to take action to overcome them. You can scale the mountain or go around it, reduce it to a molehill with dynamite or dig a tunnel straight through it. Expect trouble as an inevitable part of life. When it comes, look it squarely in the eye. You are bigger than trouble; it cannot defeat you.

Action Item: Name two strategies for problem-solving that differ from the norm.

_____

_____

_____

_____

_____

_____

_____

_____

_____

_____

_____

_____

_____

The hardest victory to achieve is the victory of one's self.

_____/_____/_____
Month   Day   Year

THE SOLUTION:
OVER, AROUND, UNDER OR THROUGH

TUESDAY:

When you seek and find a partner in a relationship that is fulfilling, it is not an easy task. Take care of yourself first. Be fulfilled, not dependent on someone else to 'make your day.' Your happiness, peace and well-being are largely your own responsibility. A relationship requires communication and compromise, but not domination and control.

Reflection: What is your reality check as it relates to relationships?

_____

_____

_____

_____

_____

_____

_____

_____

_____

_____

_____

_____

_____

_____

_____

Before sharing your life with another,
be certain that you understand yourself.

THE SOLUTION:
OVER, AROUND, UNDER OR THROUGH

Do you feel a need to be in a relationship? Honestly and unapologetically, assess your own expectations. Move forward with the expectation that you should begin with the end in mind. Adults, in particular, don't tend to change. Therefore, knowing yourself and taking your partner 'as they are' might just be your best beginning. If change is needed and change comes, then good for you. If not, you had no expectation.

Reflection: We teach what we know. We reproduce ourselves by who we attract.

_____

_____

_____

_____

_____

_____

_____

_____

_____

_____

_____

_____

_____

People advising others often forget that the same advice applies to their life as well.

_____/_____/_____
Month   Day   Year

THE SOLUTION:
OVER, AROUND, UNDER OR THROUGH

THURSDAY:

Believe in yourself. It is very important that you remain task-oriented.
You must find a way to complete the task, fulfill the challenge, accomplish the
project, and learn the value add of bringing initiatives to closure. It is critical
that you find a way...if not, you will find an excuse. You can find a way through
misery, humor or passion.

Reflection: Think about it. Love finds a way!

_____

_____

_____

_____

_____

_____

_____

_____

_____

_____

_____

_____

_____

"I believe that life is given to us so we may grow in love...
the Light in my darkness, the Voice in my silence."
- Helen Adams Keller

THE SOLUTION:
Over, Around, Under Or Through

To achieve the best is not an easy task. When building, you must seek to use the best materials. The greatest encounter with obstacles can turn into opportunities for you to shine, grow and thrive. In life, you have and will always have a fresh chance to make the world a better place. What is your plan of action?

Reflection: A dead end can never be a one-way street; you can always turn around and take another road.

_____

_____

_____

_____

_____

_____

_____

_____

_____

_____

_____

_____

_____

_____

Patience should walk side by side with wisdom.

_____/_____/_____
Month Day Year

245

THE SOLUTION:
Over, Around, Under Or Through

SATURDAY:

There is a crab-in-the barrel syndrome. Advisedly, you should not wait for the cure. If there is single crab in the barrel, it will find a way to climb up and out on its own. If, however, there are a dozen crabs in a barrel, be assured, that 11 will use all of their energy to pull down the single crab who has the determined spirit to rise to the top. Insecure people will always try to find a way to bring others down. Sound familiar?

Action Item: Identify a situation when you were seeking to excel, and others were pulling you down. How did you overcome?

_____

_____

_____

_____

_____

_____

_____

_____

_____

_____

_____

_____

"The greatest part of our happiness depends on our dispositions,
not our circumstances."
- Martha Washington

September

Relationship

"Don't wait around for other people to be happy for you. Any happiness you get you've got to make yourself."
—Alice Walker

DENIAL IS MORE THAN A RIVER IN EGYPT

SUNDAY:

The Nile River in Egypt often gets referenced when people are dealing with denial. They state, mistakenly, 'de-nial,' which sounds like 'the Nile.' Just in case you are in denial, and you have not been realistic about something that's happening in your life–face the fact.

Reflection: Think about it, name two realities that you have denied for at least the last three years.

_____

_____

_____

_____

_____

_____

_____

_____

_____

_____

_____

_____

_____

_____

Sometimes you just have to face the truth. It is unavoidable.

_____

DENIAL IS MORE THAN A RIVER IN EGYPT

Denial is simply refusing to acknowledge that an event has occurred. The person affected simply acts as if nothing has happened, behaving in ways that others may see as bizarre.

Action Item: List three things that have made you act as if there has been no change in a relationship or in a situation, circumstance or event.

_____

_____

_____

_____

_____

_____

_____

_____

_____

_____

_____

_____

_____

The future you see for yourself is the future you get.

_____/_____/_____
Month   Day   Year

DENIAL IS MORE THAN A RIVER IN EGYPT

TUESDAY:

Sufferers may be as mystified by the behavior of others as those same people are about their own behavior. It may be that you are 'turning a blind eye' to an uncomfortable situation. You lose a loved one and yet, you refuse to believe that they have gone.

Reflection: When have you had the greatest difficulty in releasing that which you hoped was not true? List three things that have made you act as if there has been no change in a relationship or in a situation, circumstance or event.

_____

_____

_____

_____

_____

_____

_____

_____

_____

_____

_____

_____

_____

Denial can relate to refusing to face grief or any bad news.
Don't be a victim. Face it.

_____/_____/_____
Month   Day   Year

DENIAL IS MORE THAN A RIVER IN EGYPT

People take credit for their successes and find 'good reason' for their failures, blaming the situation on somebody else or on other people, etc. Those who are addicted, deny that they have a problem. Optimists deny that things may go wrong. Pessimists deny they may succeed, and the list goes on.

Reflection: Classify yourself, and make a decision when you have been the most unrealistic and/or unaccepting of reality.

_____

_____

_____

_____

_____

_____

_____

_____

_____

_____

_____

_____

_____

The harder you fall, the higher you bounce.

_____/_____/_____
Month   Day   Year

DENIAL IS MORE THAN A RIVER IN EGYPT

THURSDAY:

When you deny a situation, then the other person may join you in the denial or fail to handle the situation in a direct manner. When people don't want to accept or admit that they made a mistake, when they didn't follow directions or can't understand what action is being requested or admit the truth, a true assessment is required. It is true, "Denial is more than a river in Egypt."

Reflection: Are you being held hostage by denial? How can you improve?

_____

_____

_____

_____

_____

_____

_____

_____

_____

_____

_____

_____

_____

Sometimes we stare so long at a door that is closing,
that we miss the door that is open.

DENIAL IS MORE THAN A RIVER IN EGYPT

Denial is an unconscious process. What is that you are denying? Have you decided that someone does not matter, and they actually do? Is it a circumstance, a proposal, an evaluation in the workplace or a grade in school? Speak the truth to yourself.

Action Item: The phrase is accurate, "You cannot fix it, if you cannot face it." What have you mentally framed as something that just did not happen or has not changed?

_____

_____

_____

_____

_____

_____

_____

_____

_____

_____

_____

_____

Seek the company of like-minded people. If not, consider whether they need to be on your invitation list.

253

DENIAL IS MORE THAN A RIVER IN EGYPT

SATURDAY:

A hint to the wise should be sufficient. Be certain that you are not playing a waiting game whether the issue relates to your personal health, a job situation, or a relationship. Don't wait. When you are moving from the position of denial, you could easily become the headwaiter in line.

Action Item: Refresh your mental health and well-being. Give yourself a mental and emotional spa treatment. Cleanse. Simply put, what is it that you need to face?

_____

_____

_____

_____

_____

_____

_____

_____

_____

_____

_____

_____

_____

_____

Take advantage of the fact that you can shape your destiny.

WHEN YOU THINK ALL IS LOST, IT ISN'T

When you are pre-occupied with the thought that there is no hope. There is.

Action Item: List the time when you were convinced hope was gone. How did you regain your belief that hope returns and success can be yours?

_____

_____

_____

_____

_____

_____

_____

_____

_____

_____

_____

_____

_____

_____

Live your life with hope in your heart.

_____/_____/_____
Month   Day   Year

WHEN YOU THINK ALL IS LOST, IT ISN'T

MONDAY:

Hope triumphs over worry, frustration, anxiety and disappointment. When you have lost everything, there is always hope.

Action Item: List three of your greatest losses. Why?

_____

_____

_____

_____

_____

_____

_____

_____

_____

_____

_____

_____

_____

Hope is a good thing.

WHEN YOU THINK ALL IS LOST, IT ISN'T

Life deals each of us a full deck of things to handle. Many will be unpleasant, and some will seem impossible. Marriage vows will be given and broken; children who could have and should have excelled, disappoint; when everything you hold dear seems to crumble all around you; investments will be made and lost; beloved ones will transition and, at first, you may be convinced that your life will be shattered. But it won't.

Reflection: Life is lived in stages. Think of a time when you learned that, '...this, too, shall pass.'

_____

_____

_____

_____

_____

_____

_____

_____

_____

_____

_____

_____

_____

_____

_____

If you expect nothing, you will never be disappointed.

257

_____/_____/_____
Month   Day   Year

WHEN YOU THINK ALL IS LOST, IT ISN'T

WEDNESDAY:

You may have solid expectations about what life owes you. Life owes you nothing. Every day it is required that you not only face, but overcome, even the most difficult task.

Reflection: What made you realize that life gives you no entitlement(s)?

_____

_____

_____

_____

_____

_____

_____

_____

_____

_____

_____

_____

_____

_____

Live beyond what you think you are capable of...yes,
you can do this.

WHEN YOU THINK ALL IS LOST, IT ISN'T

THURSDAY:

Whether the journey is taken with ease or desperation, you reach the same destination. Just like a plane ride, you have to make a decision in what class you want to ride—first class, business class or coach. The ride is different. The choice is yours.

Reflection: What life section do you choose for yourself? Why?

_____

_____

_____

_____

_____

_____

_____

_____

_____

_____

_____

_____

Use your life experiences to make rational decisions.

_____/_____/_____
Month   Day   Year

WHEN YOU THINK ALL IS LOST, IT ISN'T

FRIDAY:

Take up residence with hope. Be big enough to love. It makes us better than we are. Your outreach to others will live beyond your lifetime. Those things that you do just for yourself, live just for your lifetime. If you chose to believe, love, and help others, you are also making a decision to live far beyond your years.

Action Item: Give two examples of your community outreach, and how you felt as a result of giving your time, talent and resources.

_____

_____

_____

_____

_____

_____

_____

_____

_____

_____

_____

_____

_____

_____

If you want to help yourself, first, help somebody else.

___ / ___ / ___
Month   Day   Year

260

WHEN YOU THINK ALL IS LOST, IT ISN'T

Trust me, you will be alright. Life offers many good things that make life worth living. Be positive. Be a realist. Embrace hope, promise, love and kindness like a long time friend. You have a lot to enjoy and experience. If you are reading this, and writing in your daily journal, you are alive and above ground. Celebrate! You have a fantastic reason!

Action Item: Do you have an attitude of gratitude? Explain why?

_____

_____

_____

_____

_____

_____

_____

_____

_____

_____

_____

_____

Don't worry...whatever you are going through,
in the end, everything will work out.

_____/_____/_____
Month   Day   Year

THE GAMES PEOPLE PLAY

SUNDAY:

In friendship, you have to make a decision as to whether your standard for a friendship is too high, or just enough. Is the friendship a banner or a burden? Are you emotionally, mentally and spiritually secure enough to look at friendship with a win, lose or draw attitude? In other words, whatever occurs, you are fine-notwithstanding. True friendship speaks the truth to your heart.

Reflection: Identify three best friends in your life. Were your friendships continual or did they change during the various stages of your life?

_____

_____

_____

_____

_____

_____

_____

_____

_____

_____

_____

_____

_____

_____

_____

When everything is fine, your friends are present;
when everything isn't, you discover who your friends are.

THE GAMES PEOPLE PLAY

MONDAY:

The older we get and more successful we become, we have new obligations and responsibilities. We work longer hours; we build families and must accommodate their needs, wants and expectations. Children have homework, sports events and concerts, too. Our need to excel at work, is not erased by the need mandate to fix things around the house, run errands, and, to be the caretaker or counselor for an ailing family member.

Reflection: What are your requirements for friendship in view of the fact it may be true that 'your time is already limited.'

_____

_____

_____

_____

_____

_____

_____

_____

_____

_____

_____

_____

_____

If you think your friends have changed, they will prove it.

263

_____/_____/_____
Month   Day   Year

THE GAMES PEOPLE PLAY

TUESDAY:

It is true, that we can pick friends and not family. When friends do something that is unexpected, it can knock us for a loop. The range of disappointments can include, being absent when you counted on them for support; for them to tell the truth, as opposed to spreading a lie; when a friend remained quiet when they should have spoken up for you; as a result, your trust was destroyed.

Action Item: List two times a 'true friend' destroyed your trust.

_____

_____

_____

_____

_____

_____

_____

_____

_____

_____

_____

_____

_____

_____

If a friendship ends, it never existed.

_____

_____/_____/_____
Month   Day   Year

264

THE GAMES PEOPLE PLAY

People play games with feelings. Simply put, it is not the thing to do.

Reflection: Do you think that you have intentionally orchestrated your friendship with another person to ensure your own advantage? What was the result?

_____

_____

_____

_____

_____

_____

_____

_____

_____

_____

_____

Remember this...you will be able to always recall what a friend did to you. Imagine that!

265

/ /
Month   Day   Year

THE GAMES PEOPLE PLAY

THURSDAY:

Your feelings are crushed, because you are on the wrong side of the VIP rope. You felt confused, angry or betrayed. Looking back, your one-time friend betrayed you more than once or twice. You said nothing and took no action. Under the guise of friendship, you let it pass, ignored it completely or surmised that your friend really didn't mean it.

Reflection: How have your altered your friendship, when you have felt betrayed?

_____

_____

_____

_____

_____

_____

_____

_____

_____

_____

_____

_____

_____

_____

_____

_____

If you are wondering whether you can actually trust a person,
you probably can't.

THE GAMES PEOPLE PLAY

While there are lifelong friendships that are treasured, there are other friendships that are negative, destructive, or unhealthy.

Action Item: Name three qualities that support wholesome friendships.

_____

_____

_____

_____

_____

_____

_____

_____

_____

_____

_____

_____

_____

_____

_____

_____

For some, a failed friendship is analogous to a failed marriage.

_____/_____/_____
Month   Day   Year

THE GAMES PEOPLE PLAY

SATURDAY:

Communicate. Raise and discuss your issues. Then, move on. Adults rarely change, but you will know who and what you are working with. True friendship offers promise and certainty.

Action Item: List three qualities required by an individual who has a commitment to friendship.

_____

_____

_____

_____

_____

_____

_____

_____

_____

_____

_____

_____

When your friendship hits a brick wall, you have a new frame of reference for whether and how your friendship will survive.

THE RELATIONSHIP:
AFTER THE HONEYMOON

Marriage is a funny thing, scary or romantic…or not? Anybody who has not been married cannot give a clear explanation about marriage. Very often, people who have been married are incapable of defining it. The actual meaning of marriage evolves with shifting values and that which is considered to be essential.

Reflection: Marriage is a real job 24/7. You have to decide whether it is a job worth working.

_____

_____

_____

_____

_____

_____

_____

_____

_____

_____

_____

_____

The success of marriage comes not in finding the 'right' person,
but in adjusting to the real person you married.

_____/_____/_____
Month   Day   Year

THE RELATIONSHIP:
AFTER THE HONEYMOON

MONDAY:

Marriage is often defined as the ultimate proof for the love between two people. It is related to words like 'forever,' 'together,' 'sharing,' 'loyalty,' and children. For some, marriage is a formality, required for this society. The irony is that all of these things, and more, may exist simultaneously.

Reflection: Does marriage interfere with romance?

_____

_____

_____

_____

_____

_____

_____

_____

_____

_____

_____

_____

_____

_____

To be married just to be married would be lonelier than
spending the rest of your life with someone you couldn't talk to,
or worse.

TUESDAY:

Marriage is the final step when two people decide to spend their lives together. Yet, if two people are really sure that they want to spend the rest of their lives with each other, then marriage is really permanent, from the beginning. If that is true, why doesn't this formula work?

Reflection: "Love is a temporary insanity curable by marriage."

_____

_____

_____

_____

_____

_____

_____

_____

_____

_____

_____

_____

*There can be no disparity in marriage
like unsuitability of mind and purpose.*

_____/_____/_____
Month   Day   Year

THE RELATIONSHIP:
AFTER THE HONEYMOON

WEDNESDAY:

If he's not calling you, it's because you are not on his mind. If he creates expectations for you, and then doesn't follow through on little things, he will do the same for big things. Recognize when he is just fine with disappointing you. If he's choosing not to make a simple effort that would put you at ease and bring harmony to a recurring fight, then he doesn't respect your feelings and needs.

Reflection: Think about it, second is not first, it is second. This is fact, not rocket science.

_____

_____

_____

_____

_____

_____

_____

_____

_____

_____

_____

_____

_____

_____

Be remembered by your partner.

_____

THE RELATIONSHIP:
AFTER THE HONEYMOON

You know it's never fifty-fifty in a marriage. It's always seventy-thirty, or sixty-forty. Someone falls in love first. Someone puts someone else up on a pedestal. Someone works very hard to keep things rolling smoothly; someone else sails along for the ride.

Reflection: Which person are you? Are you willing to work on bringing equality to the union?

_____

_____

_____

_____

_____

_____

_____

_____

_____

_____

_____

_____

_____

It is not a lack of love, but a lack of friendship that
makes unhappy marriages.

_____/_____/_____
Month   Day   Year

THE RELATIONSHIP:
AFTER THE HONEYMOON

FRIDAY:

People always fall in love with the most perfect aspects of each other's personalities. Anybody can love the most wonderful parts of another person. But that's not the clever trick. The question is, whether you accept their flaws.

Reflection: The grass is greener, when it is watered.

_____

_____

_____

_____

_____

_____

_____

_____

_____

_____

_____

_____

_____

_____

_____

Either you win or the relationship wins.

THE RELATIONSHIP:
AFTER THE HONEYMOON

Often people marry with the hope and even anticipation that their partner will never change. Prepare for the inevitable disappointment.

Reflection: Marriage is a fine institution, but are you ready for an institution.

_____

_____

_____

_____

_____

_____

_____

_____

_____

_____

_____

_____

_____

People get married to have a witness to their lives. In marriage,
you care about the good things, the bad things, the terrible
things, and the mundane things-everyday.

_____/_____/_____
Month   Day   Year

October

Relationships II

*"Whatever is bringing you down, get rid of it.
Because you'll find that when you're free…your true self comes out."*
—Tina Turner

WHAT IS SO GOOD ABOUT GOODBYE?

Popularized by the singing group, recorded by R&B group 1961 The Miracles for Motown Records and later Temptations, written by William 'Smokey' Robinson: *"What's so good about goodbye. All it does is make me cry. Well if leavin' causes grievin'...And to part will break your heart...Tell me what's so good about it...I could've done without it...What's so good about goodbye...Since you said goodbye to me...All I know is misery...Well if everything goes wrong...When two lovers say so long...Tell me what's so good about it...I could've done without it..What's so good about goodbye..."*

Action Item: Identify two occasions in your life when you felt the satisfaction or pain of saying 'goodbye.'

_____

_____

_____

_____

_____

_____

_____

_____

_____

_____

_____

_____

Keep an open mind. Few things in life are eternal.

_____/_____/_____
Month   Day   Year

277

WHAT IS SO GOOD ABOUT GOODBYE?

MONDAY:

When situations are ending, work, relationships or life itself for a loved one, engage in conversations so that you are not left wishing that you shared your thoughts before the end. In the case of death and dying, Ira Byock, author of The Four Things That Matter Most: 'Please forgive me.' 'I forgive you.' 'Thank you.' 'I love you.' Saying good-bye doesn't come naturally to most adults.

Reflection: When saying goodbye to a loved one, how did you feel about your conversations? If there was no opportunity to share, how did you overcome their absence?

_____

_____

_____

_____

_____

_____

_____

_____

_____

_____

_____

_____

_____

_____

_____

_____

Life is phenomenal.

_____

WHAT IS SO GOOD ABOUT GOODBYE?

Bringing closure may often be discussed as if a person is living in two different worlds. They may speak about risk, taking a journey, going on a trip, or an adventure. It is to bring to an end what they know now, to go to something or to somewhere unknown.

Reflection: If someone asked you to pack a bag for an extended trip and you had no additional details, what would you pack and why?

_____

_____

_____

_____

_____

_____

_____

_____

_____

_____

_____

_____

_____

Live a purposeful life, so that at the end,
your options are not limited.

279

WHAT IS SO GOOD ABOUT GOODBYE?

WEDNESDAY:

Be realistic in your conversation. Those who are facing major change or transition, neither need nor want someone who is engaged in make believe. They appreciate honesty, realism and understanding. These attributes give comfort, not confusion. A different approach ignores the obvious and it becomes analogous to refusing to acknowledge the 'elephant in the room.'

Action Item: Identify two times when you talked around the subject rather than being forthcoming and honest.

_____

_____

_____

_____

_____

_____

_____

_____

_____

_____

_____

_____

_____

_____

_____

_____

Speak directly, not hypothetically, about change and transition.

___/___/_____
Month Day   Year

WHAT IS SO GOOD ABOUT GOODBYE?

You have fallen in love and have decided that you have met your soul-mate. For a while, you felt wonderful, and then, challenged. No, you were not anticipating a perfect fit, but at least you expected more peace, than problems. No relationship is perfect. Ending a long-term relationship, also involves shared time, memories and special occasions.

Reflection: It is important for you to understand what went wrong, how and why—mentally, physically, emotionally and spiritually. There will be a next time. Don't be afraid, just be prepared.

_____

_____

_____

_____

_____

_____

_____

_____

_____

_____

_____

_____

_____

After a while of being upset and faced with daily bitter
exchanges, consider what the sailor does, escape it.

281

WHAT IS SO GOOD ABOUT GOODBYE?

FRIDAY:

Human beings want and need love. In return, we give love to others. We all need someone to love and to be loved by someone. A long-term relationship provides you with the familiarity of a routine, trust and someone to share; gives you the stability of just that with one person whom you can trust and share your hopes, dreams, wishes and intimacy.

Action Item: If you were to name your relationship book, what title would you select? What story would you write about your relationship?

_____

_____

_____

_____

_____

_____

_____

_____

_____

_____

_____

_____

_____

_____

_____

_____

In a relationship, be very committed to the fact that you are not going to let the negatives outweigh the positives.

WHAT IS SO GOOD ABOUT GOODBYE?

Saying good-bye to a bad friend or a deteriorated relationship that needs to end may not be easy, but it is necessary. Things happen. People change. Circumstances alter. People move and they lose touch with those who were once very important in their lives. Let your relationships, whether romantic or a friendship, be empowering, enriching and uplifting. If not, determine whether you need to be stressed, depressed or have your own emotional state constantly subjected to will of another.

Action Item: Describe two instances when long-term relationships in your life were changed. What was your exit strategy?

_____

_____

_____

_____

_____

_____

_____

_____

_____

_____

_____

_____

_____

In a relationship, seek the authenticity that results in joy,
comfort and the quality time of sharing one with the other.

_____/_____/_____
Month   Day   Year

283

THIS, TOO, SHALL PASS

SUNDAY:

"'It is to expect nothing, to wonder at nothing that is done to me, to feel nothing done against me. It is to be at rest when nobody praises me, and when I am blamed or despised...(at) peace as in a deep sea of calmness, when all around and above is trouble." –Andrew Murray

Reflection: There is music in words. Listen. Hear. Think.

_____

_____

_____

_____

_____

_____

_____

_____

_____

_____

_____

_____

_____

"When we speak, we are afraid our words will not
be heard or welcomed. But when we are silent,
we are still afraid. So it is better to speak."
–Audre Lorde

THIS, TOO, SHALL PASS

You are empowered to achieve the best of the human freedoms. You can select your own attitude in each of life's circumstances. There are multiple wonders in life. You have an endless opportunity to go, see and do the many things that await. There is no time for isolation from the experiences of the world. You have people to meet and things to explore, worldwide. Go Forward.

Reflection: Has your attitude changed toward reaching beyond doing the same things with the same people as you have matured or not?

_____

_____

_____

_____

_____

_____

_____

_____

_____

_____

_____

_____

"Don't compromise yourself. You are all you've got."
–Janis Joplin

_____/_____/_____
Month   Day   Year

THIS, TOO, SHALL PASS

TUESDAY:

Whatever you chose to do, it is your choices that show who you truly are. You strive to attain and maintain your abilities. It is your decision-making that is most important. Be courageous and patient, as well. Be surrounded by peace at the end of each day.

Action Item: List three times when you worked with patience, rather than controversy, and found that you were the victor.

_____

_____

_____

_____

_____

_____

_____

_____

_____

_____

_____

If you expect nothing, you will never be disappointed.

THIS, TOO, SHALL PASS

Don't get upset about the fact that you cannot orchestrate how others will shape their lives or how they will live their lives. All you can really do is to live your life. You can try to be an exemplary example that makes you and those who know you, proud. Whatever you do in life does not depend upon whether you did a great job with a fantastic hand of cards. Instead, the tougher assignment is to win the game of life, with a poor playing hand.

Reflection: Have you ever felt that the deck was stacked against you, and you excelled, anyway?

_____

_____

_____

_____

_____

_____

_____

_____

_____

_____

_____

_____

*"Real change comes when you focus on
yourself—not on changing him..."*
–Dory Hollander

_____/_____/_____
Month   Day   Year

THIS, TOO, SHALL PASS

Thursday:

THURSDAY:

The past cannot be changed, but it can be forgiven. Accordingly, it is significant to know that everything that comes your way is temporary. Nothing lasts eternally, always and forevermore. Pain will come, and go. Hurt will heal. Joy will bring a time of celebration, as well as become fleeting; for it, too, shall pass away.

Reflection: Evaluate your situations, but know that whatever they are, good or bad, they will not last.

_____

_____

_____

_____

_____

_____

_____

_____

_____

_____

_____

_____

_____

_____

_____

Celebrate health, happiness, peace and an abundance of life.

THIS, TOO, SHALL PASS

Too many people today know the price of everything and the value of nothing.

Reflection: Some people are so poor that all they have is money.

_____

_____

_____

_____

_____

_____

_____

_____

_____

_____

_____

"Never let a problem to be solved
become more important than a person to be loved."
- Barbara Johnson

_____/_____/_____
Month   Day   Year

289

THIS, TOO, SHALL PASS

SATURDAY:

Forgiveness does not change the past, but it does enlarge the future. When you are seeking enrichment and betterment for yourself, you must be willing to lay any and all things on the table that may be holding you back. If you are carrying a grudge, or holding fast to that 'Never Again!' sign, or being determined that the person you have decided to 'hate' for the rest of your life, is present in your life, let it go. They don't deserve to be on your radar screen. Your thoughts take time, and impede your success.

Reflection: You deserve a break from the person and/or situation that is holding your back.

_____

_____

_____

_____

_____

_____

_____

_____

_____

_____

_____

_____

_____

_____

_____

A flower has to go through a lot of dirt before it can bloom.

_____

PASSAGES

At one time, the cautionary admonition of 'acting your age' had a real meaning. It was easier to place one within an age group and to determine how they should act, work and play. There were certain expectations that accompanied an age group. For example, going to college, leaving home, getting married, having children and retiring took place at anticipated times in one's life cycle. Things have changed.

Action Item: Identify three situations when you have misclassified another person's age. Name the factors that made you miss the mark.

_____

_____

_____

_____

_____

_____

_____

_____

_____

_____

_____

_____

_____

"The true meaning of life is to plant trees,
whose shade you do not expect to sit."
– G. K. Chesterton

_____/_____/_____
Month   Day   Year

PASSAGES

MONDAY:

Today, we have the Millennials, Generations X and Y, the baby boomers, and more. We have women who have decided even though they are over 40, they want to be 'cougars' and date younger men. Those whom many thought had missed their window to obtain a college degree discovered that it is never too late. Instead, seniors, 80 and above are marching across the stage to receive their doctorate degree.

Action Item: Name four major changes that indicate the 'then and now' of change.

_____

_____

_____

_____

_____

_____

_____

_____

_____

_____

_____

_____

_____

_____

U.S. Census, 2012 Statistical Abstract, National Data Book,
reports that by 2015, the life expectancy for men will be 76.4
and for females, it will be, 81.4 years of age.

_____/_____/_____
Month   Day   Year

PASSAGES

Life events have changed. Based upon an ever-increasing life expectancy, people believe that they can do what they want to do, when they want to do it. They are not bound by any constraints on what should happen at a certain age. Definitions of the young and seasoned become interchangeable depending upon the person.

Reflection: "The truth is rarely pure and never simple." —Oscar Wilde

_____

_____

_____

_____

_____

_____

_____

_____

_____

_____

_____

_____

_____

_____

Real beauty is realized in a person as they get older.

_____/_____/_____
Month   Day   Year

293

PASSAGES

WEDNESDAY:

If the new 60 is actually, 40; and the new 50 is actually 30; then can it be that the new 70 is actually 50? This is the time when we see grandmothers under 40 and great grandmothers very short of 55, and few raise their eyebrows. People go to school, marry and/or work; they retire, and then, work at the same job again, as a consultant, making more money than they did as a salaried employee.

Reflection: Older can be viewed as better.

The two hardest things to handle in life are failure and success.

PASSAGES

To know how to grow old is a work of wisdom, and one of the most difficult passages in the art of living. When you are young, you run into difficulties. When you are older, difficulties, it seems, run into you. Listen to your life.

Reflection: Our thoughts are what make the universe in which we live, move and have our being. Age and aging is whatever you think they are. You are as old as you think.

_____

_____

_____

_____

_____

_____

_____

_____

_____

_____

_____

_____

*"I wish you humor and a twinkle in the eye. I wish you glory
and the strength to bear its burdens. I wish you sunshine on your
path and storms to season your journey."*
– Robert A. Ward

295

PASSAGES

Everyday has its own level of importance. Do not disregard a day in your life. Use it, with purpose. 'To laugh often and much; to win the respect of intelligent people and the affection of children; to earn the appreciation of honest criticism and endure the betrayal of false friends; to appreciate beauty and find the best in others; to leave this world a better place whether by a healthy child, a garden patch, a redeemed social condition; to know even one life has breathed easier because you have lived—this is to have succeeded."
–Ralph Waldo Emerson

Action Item: Identify two ways in which you are keeping the child inside yourself, alive.

_____

_____

_____

_____

_____

_____

_____

_____

_____

_____

_____

_____

_____

"There is nothing noble about being superior to some other man.
The true nobility is in being superior to your previous self."
–Hindu Proverb

PASSAGES

If age is just a number, then it is necessary to consider the components of one's attitude, behavior, goals and achievements. Aging is a total of our life experiences. "People of age object too much, consult too long, adventure too little, repent too soon and seldom drive business home to its conclusion, but content themselves with a mediocrity of success." –Francis Bacon.

Reflection: Neither age nor aging is a disease.

_____

_____

_____

_____

_____

_____

_____

_____

_____

_____

_____

_____

_____

*The truly important things in life – love, beauty, and one's own
uniqueness – are constantly being overlooked.*

_____/_____/_____
Month   Day   Year

THE STORM IS PASSING OVER

SUNDAY:

Events can frame life experiences in such a way that you know you are, in fact, in a storm. Your routine is altered and, most likely, forever changed. Your frame of reference is shaped by that shifting set of circumstances that helped you to know and accept, that what you thought would never be, was exactly what happened, not to somebody else, but to you and yours. It was a storm pounding against your life.

Action Item: When did you experience an unexpected storm in your life? How did you handle it?

_____

_____

_____

_____

_____

_____

_____

_____

_____

_____

_____

_____

_____

_____

_____

Remember: "Laugh, and the world laughs with you;
Weep, and you weep alone."
– Ella Wheeler-Wilcox

THE STORM IS PASSING OVER

Be reminded that in life, there are three groups of people-those who are just getting out of a storm, those who are in the midst of the storm and those who are getting ready to go into the storm. In life's struggles, sacrifices and challenges depends upon the foundation upon which you have built your life.

Reflection: When you are left without words, collect the silence and become introspective.

_____

_____

_____

_____

_____

_____

_____

_____

_____

_____

_____

_____

With the storms in your life,
to let them pass, you must let them go.

_____/_____/_____
Month   Day   Year

THE STORM IS PASSING OVER

TUESDAY:

As a decision maker, you have the responsibility of accepting the fact that your choices determine your circumstances. A storm can mold and shape you. At the time, it may be more than inconvenient; it can be painful, upsetting, disturbing and hurtful.

Reflection: Think about whether you have ever seen a storm that did not pass over.

_____

_____

_____

_____

_____

_____

_____

_____

_____

_____

_____

_____

_____

_____

"Memory is a way of holding on to the things you love, the things you are, the things you never want to lose."
—Flora Whittlemore

THE STORM IS PASSING OVER

When the weather is overcast and cloudy, people tend to rush to get home, seek shelter from the storm and to express verbally how harrowing it is to be in a storm. At the first signs of the storm passing over, there is relief, comfort and joy. And, there is an attitude of gratitude that there is a brighter day ahead. You will have an encouraged spirit that things are going to get better once the storm moves on, and it will.

Reflection: You know my name, not my story.

_____

_____

_____

_____

_____

_____

_____

_____

_____

_____

_____

_____

_____

_____

"Expect trouble as an inevitable part of life, and when it comes,
hold your head high, look it squarely in the eye and say, 'I will be
bigger than you. You cannot defeat me.'
– Ann Landers

_____/_____/_____
Month   Day   Year

THE STORM IS PASSING OVER

THURSDAY:

Storms actually teach lessons. The thunder, tumultuous winds and whirlwinds, and often-unceasing rain can give you a new perspective as well as a longing for the peace and calm that reigned before the storm. Storms demonstrate that you are not in charge, when nature takes over. A storm neutralizes the warrior and the one who is passive and accepting, alike. Both must simply wait out the storm.

Reflection: Be certain to look at life through the windshield, not through the rear view mirror.

The difference between school and life: In school, you're taught a lesson and then given a test. In life, you're given a test that teaches you a lesson.

THE STORM IS PASSING OVER

Life seems to have a requirement, and that is to enjoy a little, and to endure a great deal.

Action Item: Name two things that you have endured that made your stronger.

_____

_____

_____

_____

_____

_____

_____

_____

_____

_____

_____

_____

_____

"Our attitude toward life determines life's attitude towards us."
—Zelda Fitzgerald

_____/_____/_____
Month   Day   Year

THE STORM IS PASSING OVER

SATURDAY:

"This is my wish for you: Comfort in difficult days, smiles when sadness intrudes, rainbows to follow the clouds, laughter to kiss your lips, sunsets to warm your heart, hugs when spirits sag, beauty for your eyes to see, friendships to brighten your being, faith so that you can believe, confidence for when you doubt, courage to know yourself, patience to accept the truth, Love to complete your life." –Oscar Wilde

Reflection: Seek the best in life by seeking knowledge, but most of all, seek wisdom.

_____

_____

_____

_____

_____

_____

_____

_____

_____

_____

_____

_____

_____

_____

Through it all, take good care of yourself.
You may live a long time.

November

Civic Engagement

"Don't let anyone speak for you, and don't rely on others to fight for you."
—Michelle Obama

STAND UP AND BE COUNTED

SUNDAY:

Changing the world in positive ways can be, and most likely will be, hard to accomplish. Moreover, it will be demanding, requiring the use of your best effort, honed skill sets, and may even be hard to endure. There is a pronounced need in the pulsing heart of any city, as individuals and businesses prioritize their own interest, ranging from work, play, profit and/or materialistic gain.

Action Item: Name two incidences in which you made a decision to be the advocate for what was right, against all odds. Why?

_____

_____

_____

_____

_____

_____

_____

_____

_____

_____

_____

_____

_____

"Women are no longer expected to stand behind a man, now,
they are very likely to stand beside him."
–Jo Dee Messina

STAND UP AND BE COUNTED

What we need to do if we are going to make an impact in our world is, first of all, to acknowledge our own strengths and weaknesses, then, have a willingness to work to strategically gain the desired result in cause related efforts. There is strength in numbers. Increasingly, we see groups who organize around their own causes and interests for their mutual benefit.

Action Item: Identify your involvement with a group and the results of working to make a difference.

_____

_____

_____

_____

_____

_____

_____

_____

_____

_____

_____

_____

_____

_____

"Reflection must be reserved for solitary hours; whenever she was alone, she gave way to it as the greatest relief..."
–Jane Austin

_____/_____/_____
Month Day Year

307

STAND UP AND BE COUNTED

TUESDAY:

When a situation is persistent, and you want to get involved, how do make a decision to do something or not? The difficulty comes in making a personal ascertainment as to whether and when you should act, be acted upon and simply, let the entire matter pass, without your intervention. Personal attacks may urge you to act, or to ignore, or to turn and walk away.

Reflection: The way you handle a challenge can seriously reflect upon your character and integrity. Your plan of action can be exemplary or a disaster. You decide.

_____

_____

_____

_____

_____

_____

_____

_____

_____

_____

_____

_____

_____

_____

No one lives life backwards. Look ahead to find your future.

STAND UP AND BE COUNTED

The society has been measurably moved to follow the clarion call for 'hope and change' as well as to engage in a new activism to share information in real time. Collectively, a focus on higher goals with more long-lasting solutions and an improved way of life.

Reflection: What have you done as a 'change agent' to contribute to your legacy?

_____

_____

_____

_____

_____

_____

_____

_____

_____

_____

_____

_____

_____

If you begin well, you are half way to your destination.

309

_____/_____/_____
Month   Day   Year

STAND UP AND BE COUNTED

THURSDAY:

Commitment to a cause is now being shown not only by marches, parades, waving flags and banners, but also by the tee shirts, uniforms, and socks that we are willing to wear. Yes, a nation also affirmed their support of a medical cause, by wearing pink ribbons, pink attire worn by many flight attendants and, pink cleats on the NFL playing field.

Action Item: Name two causes that mandate your involvement. Why?

_____

_____

_____

_____

_____

_____

_____

_____

_____

_____

_____

_____

_____

_____

Being bitter requires an escape.

_____

STAND UP AND BE COUNTED

What is needed today is a spiritual army of souls demonstrating—not militantly or aggressively, but with sincerity declared—their commitment to higher values, to God, and to a firm rejection of worldly values.

Reflection: What is the impact of your unwillingness to get involved in a worthy cause?

_____

_____

_____

_____

_____

_____

_____

_____

_____

_____

_____

"When you feel powerful, you are willing to stand up for your rights...and you're more willing to stand up and be counted."
-Margaret Cho

___/___/___
Month Day Year

STAND UP AND BE COUNTED

SATURDAY:

A woman reports her father's story, as an escapee from Germany in 1938, before Hitler gained power many people stood at the sidelines not wanting to get involved or to rock the boat. Freedoms were being taken away a little at a time and those that were not affected stood back and looked the other way. They felt the most comfortable minding their own business. And now, we know the rest of the story.

Reflection: When oppression begins should only those that are oppressed have the right to stand up and object.

_____

_____

_____

_____

_____

_____

_____

_____

_____

_____

_____

_____

_____

_____

_____

Americans fought and died for our right to simply disagree.

BREAK THE SILENCE

When there is an expectation of involvement, engagement, participation, and activism, silence is not the behavior that is helpful. If the cause requires a good offense, defense or strategy, make a difference by answering the roll call to be one in the number of those who cares.

Reflection: There is a time for silence, but not when action is required.

_____

_____

_____

_____

_____

_____

_____

_____

_____

_____

_____

_____

"Your silence will not protect you."
– Audre Lorde

___/___/___
Month Day Year

313

BREAK THE SILENCE

Monday:

MONDAY:

Silence is completely turning down the volume. It is pushing the off button. Silence affords you the chance to operate on your own agenda and let others go it alone, and find their way, even in the darkness of trouble, uncertainty, and need. Spread the joy of life, by getting involved in causes that you believe in. Whether you give goods, services or time, it all counts. Make a difference.

Reflection: In life, what you get back from what you give away is greater.

_____

_____

_____

_____

_____

_____

_____

_____

_____

_____

_____

_____

_____

The world will make room for the person who knows where they are going. Based upon your words, deeds and actions, the people will decide to follow.

____/____/____
Month Day Year

BREAK THE SILENCE

When your silence is not readily understood or accepted, then, your words will also be beyond interpretation. Where do you begin? Projects are at your fingertips. Children are hungry and unclothed, and in need of clean water, at home and abroad. Sex trafficking is at a pandemic level. Think about the number of families that you know who have been affected by any form of cancer. Innumerable women and children need coaching and tutorial services, respectively. What exactly are we doing for our troops as they transition home?

Reflection: Being involved is a no brainer—do something.

_____

_____

_____

_____

_____

_____

_____

_____

_____

_____

_____

_____

_____

_____

*Do you have the courage to do the right thing when it matters
most? Too often, the answer is, silence.*

315

_____/_____/_____
Month   Day   Year

BREAK THE SILENCE

Wednesday:

WEDNESDAY:

Sometimes, the person that you don't think you want is the one you really need. Actions always prove why words mean nothing. With a million reasons why you should go your own way, love will keep you standing there, trying to find one reason to stay.

Reflection: Listen carefully. Silence has a voice.

_____

_____

_____

_____

_____

_____

_____

_____

_____

_____

_____

_____

_____

*"I've begun to realize that you can listen to silence and learn
from it. It has a quality and a dimension all its own."*
—Chaim Potok

BREAK THE SILENCE

The time comes when you must forget what you feel, and focus upon what you deserve. Remember you may not be rejecting another, you, actually, may be protecting yourself.

Reflection: In a relationship silence is two-sided: to be able to talk to another, or to simply be quiet.

_____

_____

_____

_____

_____

_____

_____

_____

_____

_____

_____

_____

_____

Words may sting, but silence is what breaks the heart.

_____/_____/_____
Month   Day   Year

BREAK THE SILENCE

FRIDAY:

Silence has a sound. The true blessing in life is to be involved in a passionate pursuit that makes a difference for others. It is to live life with a worthy purpose. Purpose serves as a principle around which to organize your life. Great minds have purposes. Small minds have wishes.

Reflection: Recall the worthy cause(s) in which you have participated that made you proud.

_____

_____

_____

_____

_____

_____

_____

_____

_____

_____

_____

_____

_____

_____

_____

We are here on earth to do good for others.
If not, why are we here?

_____/_____/_____
Month   Day   Year

318

BREAK THE SILENCE

Always remember that the purpose for which we live is the improvement of ourselves, so that we may go out of this world having lifted another, or plant a seed of good or adopt a social cause that we work to improve. Many are talking without speaking. Hearing without listening. Writing books and the content is never shared. Only the courageous will disturb the sound of silence.

Reflection: Do not speak unless you can improve the silence.

_____

_____

_____

_____

_____

_____

_____

_____

_____

_____

_____

_____

_____

_____

It isn't what you have in your pocket that makes you thankful,
but what you have in your heart.

_____/_____/_____
Month Day   Year

ENOUGH ALREADY!

SUNDAY:

Let's face it, the Golden Rule: "Do unto others as you would have them to unto you" is tarnished. The idea of civility originates in Cicero with the concept of the societas civilus-meaning that there are certain standards of conduct toward others. Common courtesy rarely exist anymore. Civility, manners, and politeness are gone. We are more mean-spirited than ever. In essence, it has become "Do unto others, and hope that they don't get around to doing unto you."

Reflection: Have you even been appropriately described as having gone 'postal?'

_____

_____

_____

_____

_____

_____

_____

_____

_____

_____

_____

_____

_____

_____

_____

_____

*A simple, 'thank you' or 'please' would make
the world a better place.*

ENOUGH ALREADY!

The examples are flagrant and continual. Significantly, the heckling of the President of the United States of America during a Joint Session of Congress by Hon. Joe Wilson (R-SC); as he refused to apologize to the House of Representatives, even though his comments were rebuked by that same decision-making body. People in positions of power and privilege have a duty to perform at a higher level.

Reflection: Is it incivility first, then, violence next?

_____

_____

_____

_____

_____

_____

_____

_____

_____

_____

_____

_____

Eight out of ten Americans believe that the failure of parents to instruct their children in good behavior is the major cause of bad manners.

_____ / _____ / _____
Month   Day   Year

ENOUGH ALREADY!

TUESDAY:

Across the spectrum of society, people are behaving badly. The issue is more complex than whether we can 'all get along?' The issue really is, whether we can co-exist, with civility. Passengers on the plane hurry to board, forgetting that everybody is going to arrive at the destination at the same time. At concerts, even though you paid $80.00 for your ticket, the whole row in front of you decides to stand up during the whole concert; and, at sporting events, people are short-tempered and rude at an epidemic level.

Reflection: Ask yourself, "Who is the standard bearer for exemplary behavior?"

_____

_____

_____

_____

_____

_____

_____

_____

_____

_____

_____

_____

_____

In the workplace, rude people are three times more likely to be in higher positions than their targets.

ENOUGH ALREADY!

Even those at the very top of their game, who are enjoying wealth and status, cannot be relied upon for ensuring a worthy example. University students demand make-up examinations and substitutions on assignments and offer creative reasons for extra credit. Professionals use cell phones in meetings; talk to each other while the leader is speaking or they decide to leave in the middle of the lecture.

Action Item: What is the impact of living in a 'toxic' atmosphere of cynicism?

_____

_____

_____

_____

_____

_____

_____

_____

_____

_____

_____

_____

_____

Compassion is America's most consequential export.

_____/_____/_____
Month   Day   Year

ENOUGH ALREADY!

THURSDAY:

Today there is a lack of respect for the chain of command; an invasion of one's work space for reasons known only to themselves, profane language and being in reception areas that are not warm or friendly as the person seeking assistance is ignored, until the employee is ready to handle your interest.

Reflection: There are those who do the work and those who take the credit.

_____

_____

_____

_____

_____

_____

_____

_____

_____

_____

_____

_____

*A kindergarten teacher instructed her students to write a letter
to the President of the United States. The last question on the
last letter read, "Are people being nice?"*

ENOUGH ALREADY!

In the workplace there is 'cubicle rage' which has people feeling pushed over the edge. Fewer people are doing more work and are crowded into smaller spaces. It is taking its toll. The cost of rudeness in business is extraordinary. Consider the reaction when customers are exposed to an employee who is inconsiderate, disrespectful or incompetent. It has become a slippery slope. Customers have choices.

Reflection: Live your life not only so that you will be remembered. Make certain that your life is worth remembering.

_Each person has the power, if they have the will,
to bring back civility._

Month   Day   Year

ENOUGH ALREADY!

SATURDAY:

The 21st century has given us an array of platforms, agendas, value statements and lapses in social conduct, behavior and responsibility. We must take heed to our silence. When we refuse to change our personal behavior or refuse to acknowledge the importance of someone else, we create the environment. Incivility is not an exception, it is an attitude. Enough Already!

Action Item: Give an example in each listed category of unacceptable attitudes or behavior—politicians, pundits, and media.

_____

_____

_____

_____

_____

_____

_____

_____

_____

_____

_____

_____

_____

_____

_____

_____

Be careful what you swallow and chew.

BE STILL

"Be still, and know that I am God." –Psalm 46:10. Whether you are a believer or not, still means, that you have permission to pause, to reflect and to renew; and, to realize that there is somebody bigger than you and me. If you are alive, everyday will not be the same. There will be ups and downs, good days and bad, successes and disappointments. Thus, you will benefit by withdrawing to think, refresh and collect your thoughts and resources.

Reflection: There is value in wrapping yourself in silence and exploring your beliefs, values and next steps.

_____

_____

_____

_____

_____

_____

_____

_____

_____

_____

_____

_____

"...I wish I had lingered a week or so...
most of us, are... forgetting that the zest is in
the journey and not in the destination."
–Ralph D. Paine

_____/_____/_____
Month   Day   Year

BE STILL

Google, the internet search engine, slowed down the responsiveness of their searches to evaluate users' reaction. Facing delays of 100 thousandths of a second, users did fewer searches. When the delay was increased to 400 thousandths of a second, the overall impact was 8 million fewer searches per day. Notably, the average blink takes about 400 thousandths of a second. Be still.

Action Item: Does the adage apply to you: "Time is money." How?

_____

_____

_____

_____

_____

_____

_____

_____

_____

_____

_____

_____

_____

Patience is a virtue.

_____/_____/_____
Month   Day   Year

BE STILL

The pace that we keep, doing one thing while thinking about another is placing us in the fast lane of life. We are stress-filled, and en route, at a faster pace, to our final resting place.

Reflection: Be still and know that God is God. Stop. Wait. Listen.

_____

_____

_____

_____

_____

_____

_____

_____

_____

_____

_____

_____

_____

Remember: Every answer does not come within seconds.

329

_____/_____/_____
Month   Day   Year

BE STILL

WEDNESDAY:

Step off the treadmill of a hurried life. There is always something to do other than living with a sense of urgency, while going from one emergency to the next. Life is short. Surely, you are tired from being the master of multi-tasking, while simultaneously adding stress to your life. You have too much to do. Ultimately, your health may become a concern.

Reflection: Make a self-assessment: Are you a human being or a human doing?

_____

_____

_____

_____

_____

_____

_____

_____

_____

_____

_____

_____

_____

_____

_____

"Nature does not hurry, yet everything is accomplished."
–Lao Tzu

_____/_____/_____
Month   Day   Year

BE STILL

You know that your pace has been/is too fast, when you reach the weekend, you still have to find a reason to get busy, to be more productive or you need to have noise around you because you simply cannot successfully, be still. You may feel exhausted, have a loss of your temper, and simply become bored, without something to do.

Action Item: Identify three ways that you can de-stress.

_____

_____

_____

_____

_____

_____

_____

_____

_____

_____

_____

_____

_____

_____

Are you convinced that you do not need a minimum of eight hours of sleep?

_____/_____/_____
Month   Day   Year

331

BE STILL

Consider a society that has gone mad in search of itself. What has happened to family/friends meals? Too often, we opt for takeout, and the conversation is business, not pleasure. People are so time-conscious that they may not know where they are going, but speed to get there. Many pursue the next thing with such haste they hurry past it.

Reflection: Just let it all go. De-clutter your mind.

If you must be in a hurry, hasten slowly.

Month   Day   Year

BE STILL

In life, all you have done is live, until you don't. Why are you in such a hurry? Along the way, there are flowers to smell, people to meet, and those who will give comfort when there is a need, places to go, and things to do, and you just may miss most of it if you simply don't have or take the time.

Reflection: Seek to achieve inner peace.

_____

_____

_____

_____

_____

_____

_____

_____

_____

_____

_____

_____

_____

_____

"If you complain about the world moving too fast, slow down."
—Mike Dolan

_____/_____/_____
Month   Day   Year

December

Against the Odds

"Life is an opportunity, benefit from it. Life is beauty, admire it.
Life is a dream, realize it. Life is a challenge, meet it.
Life is a duty, complete it. Life is a game, play it.
Life is a promise, fulfill it. Life is sorrow, overcome it.
Life is a song, sing it. Life is a struggle, accept it.
Life is a tragedy, confront it. Life is an adventure, dare it.
Life is luck, make it. Life is too precious, do not destroy it.
Life is life, fight for it."
– Mother Teresa

THE VERTICAL CONNECTION

"It is not because things are difficult that we do not dare. It is because we do not dare that they are difficult." –Seneca

A journey may be long or short, but it starts wherever you find yourself.

Reflection: The day will come when the risk to remain tight in a bud becomes more painful than the risk it takes to blossom.

_____

_____

_____

_____

_____

_____

_____

_____

_____

_____

_____

_____

_____

_____

_____

Keep your fears to yourself, but share your courage with others.

_____/_____/_____
Month   Day   Year

THE VERTICAL CONNECTION

MONDAY:

If you have made up your mind to be less than you are capable of being, then prepare to be unhappy for the rest of your life. Be courageous. Life shrinks or expands in proportion to one's courage. The only way past fear is to go through. When you leap, take a calculated risk, then, the net will appear.

Reflection: Is your life full to over-flowing or not?

_____

_____

_____

_____

_____

_____

_____

_____

_____

_____

_____

_____

_____

_____

Fear is an acronym for false evidence, appearing real.

THE VERTICAL CONNECTION

Cherish things while you still have them, before they're gone, and you realize how precious they really are. Life can only be understood backwards, but it must be lived forwards. Everything in life is temporary. So if things are going good, enjoy it because it won't last forever. And if things are going bad, don't worry because it won't last forever either. Destiny is not a matter of chance; it is a matter of choice.

Reflection: A journey of a thousand miles begins with a single step. Since you cannot add years to your life, add life to your years.

_____

_____

_____

_____

_____

_____

_____

_____

_____

_____

_____

_____

_____

"If I can stop one heart from breaking, I shall not live in vain."
—Emily Dickinson

/   /
Month   Day   Year

THE VERTICAL CONNECTION

WEDNESDAY:

Be kinder than necessary, for everyone you meet is fighting some kind of battle. Laughter is good medicine for the soul. Our world is desperately in need of more medicine. Laughter is the sun that drives winter from your face.

Action Item: Describe two features that are apparent when you laugh.

_____

_____

_____

_____

_____

_____

_____

_____

_____

_____

_____

_____

_____

"I have not ceased being fearful,
but I have ceased to let fear control me...I have gone ahead
despite the pounding that says...turn back..."
–Erica Jong

_____/_____/_____
Month Day Year

THE VERTICAL CONNECTION

Don't be afraid that your life will end, be afraid that it will never begin.

Reflection: Imagine that your life is like a closed road that forces you to turn around and find another way to your destination. Make mental notes of your discoveries.

_____

_____

_____

_____

_____

_____

_____

_____

_____

_____

_____

There is no need to crawl or even walk, when you can soar.

_____/_____/_____
Month   Day   Year

FRIDAY:

"Give the following gifts: To your enemy…forgiveness. To your opponent…tolerance. To a friend…your heart. To a customer…service. To all men…charity. To every child…a good example. To yourself…respect."
–Author Unknown

Reflection: Remain willing to contemplate life, and eternity. Think beyond what you see.

_____
_____
_____
_____
_____
_____
_____
_____
_____
_____
_____
_____
_____
_____

"Forgiveness doesn't change history;
it makes living with it easier."
–Author Unknown

THE VERTICAL CONNECTION

Each new day is a new beginning to learn more about ourselves, to care more about others, to laugh more than we did, to accomplish more than we thought we could, and be more than we were before. Live an honorable life. Then when you get older and think back, you'll be able to enjoy it a second time.

Action Item: Identify two times in your life when you have felt that you engaged in a new beginning.

_____

_____

_____

_____

_____

_____

_____

_____

_____

_____

_____

_____

_____

_____

The one who knows, and knows that she knows is wise.
Follow her.

_____/_____/_____
Month   Day   Year

TEST TO TESTIMONY

SUNDAY:

It can happen. You feel damaged beyond repair. You will not have a question as to whether you are in charge of your own life. Then you accept the fact that you are alive, if not well, because your heart hurts so much.

Reflection: Think highly of yourself, for the world takes you at your own estimate.

_____

_____

_____

_____

_____

_____

_____

_____

_____

_____

_____

_____

_____

There is no testimony, without a test.

TEST TO TESTIMONY

The reality of being bitter, hurt and distraught is not imaginary. Few people stand in line for the hurt of rejection or to face a personal tragedy for which they do not have solutions, a cure or a remedy. You ask yourself every question you can think of, what, why, how and then your sadness turns to anger. You genuinely try to figure it out, what is going on and why.

Reflection: Do not fall victim to the paralysis of analysis. Deal with what is with courage, perseverance and hope.

_____

_____

_____

_____

_____

_____

_____

_____

_____

_____

_____

_____

_____

"You've gotta dance like there's nobody watching.
Love like you'll never be hurt. Sing like there's nobody listening.
And live like it's heaven on earth."
– William W. Purkey

343

TEST TO TESTIMONY

TUESDAY:

"I hope you never lose your sense of wonder...You get your fill to eat, but always keep that hunger...May you never take one single breath for granted...God forbid love ever leaves you empty-handed. I hope you still feel small when you stand beside the ocean...Whenever one door closes, I hope one more opens...Promise me that you'll give faith a fighting chance...And when you get the choice to sit it out or dance...I hope you dance." –Lee Ann Womack

Reflection: Be careful. Worry does not empty tomorrow of its sorrow; it empties today of its strength.

_____

_____

_____

_____

_____

_____

_____

_____

_____

_____

_____

_____

_____

Dare to be courageous. Look inwardly at your own life.
Dare to be yourself.

TEST TO TESTIMONY

The truth is that our finest moments are most likely to occur when we are feeling deeply uncomfortable, unhappy, or unfulfilled. For it is only in such moments, propelled by our discomfort, that we are likely to step out of our ruts and start searching for different ways or truer answers.

Reflection: Never regret your experiences. Each one will make you a better and stronger person.

It is true, that you only live once,
but if you do it right, once is enough.

Month   Day   Year

TEST TO TESTIMONY

THURSDAY:

Remember the rainbow is beautiful, but it appears after the rain. To succeed you must first seek to improve. Then you practice, to practice you must first learn, and to learn, you must first fail. Failure is only the opportunity to begin again, this time more wisely.

Action Item: State the greatest test that you have experienced in your life. How did you overcome?

_____

_____

_____

_____

_____

_____

_____

_____

_____

_____

_____

_____

_____

_____

There is a time in the life of every problem when it is big enough to see, yet small enough to solve.

TEST TO TESTIMONY

Read every single day. May you have enough happiness to make you sweet, enough trials to make you strong, enough sorrow to keep you human, and enough hope to bring you joy.

Reflection: Nobody will believe in you, unless you believe in yourself.

_____

_____

_____

_____

_____

_____

_____

_____

_____

_____

_____

_____

"He who has health has hope,
and he who has hope has everything."
–Arabian Proverb

347

TEST TO TESTIMONY

SATURDAY:

Although at times your life journey may be crooked, winding, lonesome, and dangerous, may it also lead to the most amazing view. May your mountains rise into and above the clouds. And, may your heart be so satisfied.

Reflection: Be certain that you do not create condition precedents to your happiness or your sense of contentment. Be happy now.

_____
_____
_____
_____
_____
_____
_____
_____
_____
_____
_____
_____
_____
_____

"Life can be summarized in three words...it goes on."
– Robert Frost

VOLUNTEERISM

SUNDAY:

Volunteers make it work. They show unselfish caring, patience, a giving attitude of their time, talent and resources, they have charity in their hearts and they show love for others.

Action Item: Are you a volunteer? Explain?

_____

_____

_____

_____

_____

_____

_____

_____

_____

_____

_____

_____

_____

_____

Reach beyond your grasp. Try when you are weary.

_____/_____/_____
Month   Day   Year

VOLUNTEERISM

Monday:

MONDAY:

By learning to serve, you enrich your own life. When you give of yourself, without charge, or even expectation for compensation, others will fret, even condemn your commitment or involvement. But, they are not your record keeper. You have a higher calling.

Reflection: What is the win-win reality in volunteering?

_____

_____

_____

_____

_____

_____

_____

_____

_____

_____

_____

_____

_____

_____

_____

_____

Take the loneliness out of being alone.

_____

VOLUNTEERISM

In the search for the intentions of your heart, shine a beam of light. Somebody, whether young or seasoned, needs your hand, your smile, a few hours of your time, your help, your conversation, and your compassion.

Action Item: Describe two acts in which you have made a difference by volunteering.

_____

_____

_____

_____

_____

_____

_____

_____

_____

_____

_____

_____

_____

_____

This is your time to do all that you can,
with the limited time that you have.

_____/_____/_____
Month   Day   Year

351

VOLUNTEERISM

WEDNESDAY:

Unless someone else knows that you care, they really will not care what you know. The important thing is that neither the reward nor recognition is what really matters. The honor of giving is reward enough. Volunteering is a responsible choice.

Action Item: List three things in your life that really matter.

_____

_____

_____

_____

_____

_____

_____

_____

_____

_____

_____

_____

_____

_____

_____

_____

_____

_____

*Think about it. When you are grateful in an ungrateful world,
you actually help others.*

VOLUNTEERISM

People matter. People are to be prioritized before profits or projects. People have the mandate not only to make a living, but also to make a life. Look at it this way, a glass can be determined to be either half-empty or half full. But, a volunteer will undoubtedly make the decision that they see water in a glass and they will set out to find someone who is thirsty.

Action Item: There is thirst, hunger, or needed assistance in your community. How can you make a difference?

_____

_____

_____

_____

_____

_____

_____

_____

_____

_____

_____

_____

_____

When you help another person in a moment of despair,
you help yourself.

_____/_____/_____
Month   Day   Year

VOLUNTEERISM

FRIDAY:

Volunteers are active change agents. They are dedicated to act while there is time to empower and improve the lives of others. Many who choose the title of volunteer may not be rich in money, but they themselves, are priceless.

Action Item: A change agent versus a servant leader. Which one are you?

_____

_____

_____

_____

_____

_____

_____

_____

_____

_____

_____

_____

_____

_____

_____

Raise your voice and become essential to humankind.

VOLUNTEERISM

The human contribution is the essential ingredient. The challenge is to treat people based on what they could become, and then, help them to maximize their human potential. Advisedly, to motivate others, you must first motivate yourself. If you want to get anything done through others, you must first do it yourself.

Action Item: Do you maximize your human potential through helping others? How?

_____

_____

_____

_____

_____

_____

_____

_____

_____

_____

_____

_____

_____

Be encouraged. Be the light.
If you are here to help...grab a shovel.

_____/_____/_____
Month   Day   Year

MOUNTAIN, GET OUT OF MY WAY!

SUNDAY:

The requirement, it seems, is to move from pain, disappointment, frustration, even failure, to betterment, satisfaction, encouragement and success, respectively. Everybody goes through something. So, the challenge is to keep your eye on the mark, and press forward. Work on having the clarity, dedication and discipline to handle adversity, even through tough times. Tragedy does not need to be triumphant.

Reflection: When you were ready to give in or give up, what made you know that you could make your mountains move?

_____

_____

_____

_____

_____

_____

_____

_____

_____

_____

_____

_____

_____

Difficulties in your life don't come to destroy you,
but to help you realize your hidden potential.

MOUNTAIN, GET OUT OF MY WAY!

Even more than skill, your fortitude and perseverance can define you. With a full speed ahead spirit, you can overcome. With a true identification of the goal, and a targeted affinity for achievement you can make it. In some cases, your willingness to do so will be career altering or life-saving. Obstacles on or in your way do not have to be deterrents. Instead, they can be keys to your success.

Action Item: List three situations when you kept your eye on the goal and achieved success—anyhow.

_____

_____

_____

_____

_____

_____

_____

_____

_____

_____

_____

_____

_____

Find your something within and be your best self.

357

MOUNTAIN, GET OUT OF MY WAY!

TUESDAY:

From the beginning, know just how important you are. Move from the premise that you are worthy, that you do count, and you are critical to a situation. You are empowered to act in your best interest. Do not let others convince you that you are unequal to being your best. Be positive for yourself. Use words of affirmation. Stop entertaining negativity and letting those thoughts affect what you think that you can do. Acquaint yourself with ideas and people who overcome and who are not change resistant.

Reflection: As the person who can shape and mold your future, how confident are you about your future?

_____

_____

_____

_____

_____

_____

_____

_____

_____

_____

_____

_____

_____

_____

_____

_____

"It is time for us to stand and cheer for the doer, the achiever, the one who recognizes the challenge and does something about it."
- Vince Lombardi

MOUNTAIN, GET OUT OF MY WAY!

No obstacle is too great that it cannot be challenged—and overcome. You won't go through difficult times and the unexpected need to rise above circumstances without discovering convincing attributes that you possess to make it. Your maturity will be displayed when you demonstrate how you handle problems, adjust to the need to make decisions and refuse to be defeated.

Action Item: List two benefits you have gained from obstacles being placed in your life.

_____

_____

_____

_____

_____

_____

_____

_____

_____

_____

_____

_____

_____

"It is easier to go down a hill than up,
but the view is from the top."
- Arnold Bennett

Month Day Year

MOUNTAIN, GET OUT OF MY WAY!

THURSDAY:

Most people seek to avoid failure. People feel that they do not have the tool kit to handle missing the mark. But, you do. Failure is not catastrophic. If you are willing to be observant, it can be instructional. Failure can provide life lessons. It can give you a compass as to what not to do. Failure can return you to the drawing board to contemplate a new strategy, to find another way to make what you want to achieve, actually work. Failure is your announcement to keep on trying.

Action Item: Make a growth chart as to obstacles you have encountered and overcome. How do you assess your self-development?

_____

_____

_____

_____

_____

_____

_____

_____

_____

_____

_____

_____

_____

_____

"Well, it's a good life and a good world,
all said and done, if you don't weaken."
–Alan Sillitoe

MOUNTAIN, GET OUT OF MY WAY!

FRIDAY:

When you view a mountain as an obstacle, you should also know that each mountain has its own requirements. To overcome, reach the top, or simply climb the mountain, real or imagined, you must have multiple strategies. Understand that a mountain will not move, unless you act. Success is yours for the taking. See yourself as the one who overcomes. Do not create reasons why your success cannot be realized. Let your goal be singular, and that is, to climb the rough side of the mountain.

Action Item: Describe the time when you walked away from the mountain, and left your victory behind.

_____

_____

_____

_____

_____

_____

_____

_____

_____

_____

_____

_____

"Forgiveness doesn't change history;
it makes living with it easier."
–Author Unknown

361

_____/_____/_____
Month   Day   Year

MOUNTAIN, GET OUT OF MY WAY!

Saturday:

SATURDAY:

The word 'crisis' is from the Greek, meaning 'a moment to decide.' In life, times of challenge will vary in intensity and in duration. Typically, your challenges will also bring anxiety, fear and uncertainty. Look for the positive side in all situations. Be optimistic and not pessimistic. The reality is not what happens to you, it is the decision that you make about how you will handle what has happened to you.

Action Item: Identify three major challenges that you have experienced in your life. Describe how each one was enriching.

_____

_____

_____

_____

_____

_____

_____

_____

_____

_____

_____

_____

_____

_____

_____

_____

The one who knows, and knows that she knows is wise.
Follow her.

_____

_____/_____/_____
Month Day Year

Go in peace, prominence and prosperity...

Pat Russell-McCloud, J.D.

Patricia Russell-McCloud, J.D. is a 'visual speaking experience.' With more than 20 years on the lecture circuit, she is categorized as being one of the nation's best. Her speaking style is engaging, highly substantive, well-researched, pertinent to her audiences, entertaining, whether for the public or private sector. She is distinguished and distinct. Her style is classified as 'big, broad and animated,' which leaves her audiences anxious for more.

With each presentation she demonstrates, yet again, that she is a master at her craft as she artfully seeks to master the spoken word. In sum, this is a 'speaker's speaker' who specializes ascertaining the organization's culture, interests and challenges. The client, in turn, receives the value-add of the experience and exposure to this qualitatively measurable speaker who is, in a word—unforgettable.

Each year she speaks to more than 100,000 people in private and public organizations, both in the United States and internationally. She encourages her listeners to surmount every obstacle that stands between them and—the possible. Her client list includes, but is not limited to, AARP, National Association of Women's Business Owners; AT&T, Women's Food Service Forum, eWomen's Network, Wal-Mart/Sam's Club, General Motors, American Honda, Cox Enterprises, McDonald's, Northrop Grumman, General Electric, McGraw Hill Publishing, Memorial Sloan Kettering Cancer Center, Xerox, Procter & Gamble, and The United States Postal Service. Each company has benefited from having Russell-McCloud share her informed, inspirational wisdom and wit.

As a member of the Council on Legal Education Opportunity (CLEO), she studied at Harvard University, Cambridge, MA. She earned her Juris Doctorate degree at Howard University, School of Law, Washington, D.C. Prior to embarking upon her speaking career, Russell-McCloud was an attorney with the Federal Communications Commission, Chief, Complaints Branch, Broadcast Bureau, Washington, D.C. for ten years. Then she decided to follow her true passion which was to be a business entrepreneur and global professional orator. Born in Indianapolis, Indiana and graduating from Kentucky State University she knew that her true career connection was to prepare meaningful presentations for diverse audiences, and to meet them at their point of need.

She has received many honors, including being presented more than 300 keys to American cities. She has served as the 11th National President of The Links, Inc., and the National Parliamentarian to the Alpha Kappa Alpha Sorority, Inc. She has been named as one of the top five business motivators in the country by Black Enterprise Magazine; identified as one of the top 10 speakers in America, 'Success Runs in Our Race;' featured in ESSENCE Magazine, and in EBONY magazine as one of the most influential people in the United States, and featured as the cover story of SPEAKER magazine, National Speaker's Association 2007 July/August.

Russell-McCloud fulfills a lifelong commitment to others as a treasured mentor. "My professional journey as an attorney and international professional speaker has exposed me to many exceptional individuals who I have ultimately mentored. They are an impressive group of 145 in number, and they are primarily judges, attorneys, entrepreneurs and educators. My single requirement of them has been to 'pay it forward.' They have been responsive in their commitment to do so, and have made me deservedly proud," states Russell-McCloud.

A resident of Atlanta, Georgia, Russell-McCloud is married to Bishop E. Earl McCloud, Jr., the 127th Elected and Consecrated Bishop of the African Methodist Episcopal Church.

CPSIA information can be obtained
at www.ICGtesting.com
Printed in the USA
LVOW01*2111230217

525216LV00003B/5/P